WINES

WINES

THEIR SELECTION, CARE, AND SERVICE

WITH A *Chart of Vintage Years,* AND
OBSERVATIONS
ON *Harmonies* BETWEEN CERTAIN *Wines*
AND CERTAIN *Foods,*
AND ON *Wineglasses, Cradles, Corkscrews,* AND
KINDRED MATTERS, BY

JULIAN STREET

THIRD EDITION, *Revised* AND *Edited* BY
A. I. M. S. STREET

1 9 6 1

New York : ALFRED · A · KNOPF

L. C. catalog card number: 60-53486

1776

THIS IS A BORZOI BOOK,
PUBLISHED BY ALFRED A. KNOPF, INC.

FIRST EDITION 1933

SECOND EDITION REVISED 1948

THIRD EDITION REVISED, RESET, AND PRINTED FROM
NEW PLATES, JANUARY 1961

❧ *to a Partnership* ❧ ❧ ❧ ❧ ❧

PREFACE

This book is designed to provide a working knowledge of the world's principal wines in so far as such knowledge may be obtained without a corkscrew. It is intended to be an introduction to the corkscrew period of vinous education, and an aid thereafter.

Thanks are tendered the following persons for their generous and invaluable assistance:

Sophie Kerr, Mr. Edgar Ailes, Mr. Carl Williams, the Marquis d'Angerville, M. Chapoutier, Professor and Mrs. Pál Kelemen, Mr. and Mrs. Martin Ray, Mrs. Scoville Firuski, Mr. Robert Hawkins, Mr. William B. Brackenridge, Mr. Philip Hiaring, Mr. Kenneth Dean, Mme Fernande Garvin, and M. Georges H. Paignon.

And grateful acknowledgment is made as well to the writers on wine whose works have been freely cited, among them Mr. Philip Dexter, Mr. Charles R. Codman, Mr. P. Morton Shand, Mr. H. Warner Allen, M. André L. Simon, Mr. Philip M. Wagner, M. M. Constantin-Weyer, M. Paul de Cassagnac, MM. Cocks and Feret, Dr. Celestin Pierre Cambiaire, M. Prosper Montagné, and other French authorities, and Mr. John Melville for permission to quote from *Guide to California Wines*.

CONTENTS

CONTENTS

CONTENTS

CONTENTS

CONTENTS

Principal Vineyards of EUROPE

HOLLAND

GERMANY

POLAND

GIUM

RHEINGAU

IS

WÜRZBURGER
STEIN

CZECHO

MOSELLE

ernay

RHEINHESSEN

SLOVAKIA

AGNES

LORRAINE- PFALZ

LIS

Strassbourg

ALSACE

AUSTRIA

Dijon

TOKAY

Neuchâtel

UJOLAIS

NEUCHÂTEL

HUNGARY

Switzerland

RIESLING

ons

VALTELLINA

E-RÔTIE

VALPOLICELLA

MITAGE

PIEDMONT

BAROLO

auneuf-du-Pape

ITALY

rseille

Florence

CHIANTI

YUGOSLAVIA

EST EST EST

CASTEL
BRACCIANO

CORSICA

Rome

LACRIMA
CHRISTI-
FALERNO

Naples

Capri

SARDINIA

SEA

SICILY

Marsala

MARSALA

map by palacios

WINES

CHAPTER ONE

THE STORY OF WINE

Wine is one of the most civilized things in the world and one of the natural things of the world that has been brought to the greatest perfection, and it offers a greater range of enjoyment and appreciation than, possibly, any other purely sensory thing which may be purchased.

—ERNEST HEMINGWAY
Death in the Afternoon

ANCIENT TIMES

Excepting perhaps love and war, there is no subject in which the literature of all ages is richer than in the praise of the cup. The song of wine has been sung since the dawn of civilization, and wine itself has been peculiarly a part of civilization, for the most civilized men throughout history have used it and been loudest in acclaiming it.

Biblical references to wine are numerous, and apt and interesting quotations from the writings of the ancient Greeks and Romans about wine could be compiled into a book larger than this one. Only a passionate lover of wine could have written of it as glowingly and as understandingly as did Homer nearly a thousand years before the beginning of the Christian era. The poet Anacreon called wine "immortal," and Plato exuberantly proclaimed that "nothing more excellent than the juice of the grape was ever granted by God to man"—in which connection it is interesting to note that Anacreon, devotee of Bacchus died at the age of eighty-five by choking on a grape-seed, and that Plato, who lived to be eighty or more, died at a wedding feast.

The honor of having been the first people to make wine is variously claimed. The Persian tradition of wine-making goes back nobody knows how far into antiquity. The Chinese also claim first honors, giving the reign of the Emperor Ti-Yu, 2200 B.C., as the time of the discovery of wine; and they tell of another ancient Emperor who had the vines uprooted for fear his people would have too good a time. This prohibition by Imperial edict had such lasting effect that only in very recent years has some wine been made from grapes. The Chinese have been getting along in the interval with heavy brews made from rice and barley, or sorghum, which they call wine but which are actually distilled spirits, and various freaks such as their Tiger wine, said to have a bouquet resembling that of bone meal and to make the drinker feel and act like a tiger.

Definite knowledge as to the region inhabited by the first people to discover that grape juice, if left to itself, would ferment, marks it as the Middle East, archeologists having satisfied themselves that viticulture and wine-making were practiced in more than one spot in that area by 3000 B.C., and perhaps a thousand years earlier. The Book of Genesis relates that Noah planted a vineyard after the Flood, and from the casual tone of the passage it seems evident that his was not the first vineyard. One cannot help wondering where Noah got his grapevines; that is, whether they survived the Flood, or whether, before the Deluge, they also went into the Ark as did the animals, marching two by two.

Though the grape itself was indigenous to Europe, it appears that the art of making wine was learned from the Egyptians by the Greeks, who in turn passed it on to the Romans. The soil and climate of Sicily and Italy were so peculiarly hospitable to the vine that the Greeks named southern Italy Œnotria, or "Wineland"; and Virgil, who died in the year 19 B.C., wrote in the second book of the *Georgics* a poetic treatise on wine-growing in which he says that he who would number the wines of Italy might as well try to count the waves of the sea or the grains of sand blown by the wind upon the Libyan Desert. It was Virgil's friend Horace who left us the proverb: "Wine opens the seals of the heart."

More perhaps than to any other Roman writer we owe thanks to Pliny for what we know of the wines drunk in ancient Rome. Mr. H. Warner Allen (*The Romance of Wine*), who has delved deeper than I into the ancient history of wine, has concluded from the writings of Pliny and others that the Romans knew every trick and secret of wine-making and that, while they were not without freaks of their own, such as wine made with sea water, they had a proper appreciation of natural wine and made some wines that might very well have suited the palate of today. We know, from Pliny, that the Romans understood the art of aging wines, and that they valued certain vintage years, as we do. The fame of their Opimian year, 121 B.C., was as great in Pliny's time, nearly two hundred years later, as the fame of 1811, Year of the Comet, is in France today. Pliny tells us that in his time wine of the Opimian year was still good. It was thick like honey, and too strong to drink, but was superb when blended in small quantity with young wine.

Authorities differ as to the beginnings of wine-making in France. One affirms that the culture of wine was started in France by a colony of Greeks established at Massilia (Marseilles) about 600 B.C., whence the knowledge spread up through the Rhône Valley. It is interesting to note that the important grape of the Rhône district today, the Syrrah grape, is supposed to be descended from the Shiraz grape of ancient Persia.

The Roman influence came to French wine-growing through Cæsar's conquest of Gaul. Cæsar was a wine-lover. It is related in *The Romance of Wine* that Cæsar imported Mamertine wine from Sicily, then a foreign land, and offered it at a banquet at which "he startled the connoisseurs by serving for the first time four wines at one repast." The other three wines served at Cæsar's feast were Falernian, from what part of Italy modern savants are not sure; Lesbian, from the Ægean island of Lesbos, "where burning Sappho loved and sung"; and Chian from Chios, another island in the Ægean Sea, which, according to legend, was colonized by Œnopion, son of Bacchus, who taught the Chians viticulture so that they could impart the knowledge to the rest of mankind.

Where the Romans went they taught the "barbarians" to make wine, and thus the vineyards of Burgundy, Bordeaux, Champagne, and the Rhine came into being. The life of some of the early vineyards was not without hardship. Toward the end of the first century the Roman Emperor Domitian ordered the uprooting of all vines north of the Alps, not because he was an early "dry," but to keep them from competing with the wines of Italy, which Gibbon tells us were then world favorites. This order was not fully carried out, and by the third century the vineyards were established and had put down roots so firm that some have continued into our day. The slow-aging and excellent wine of Château Ausone, with its flavor so distinctive as to be almost a trademark, grown in the Saint Emilion region of Bordeaux, takes its name from that of the Latin Christian poet and Consul Ausonius, who was born in Burdigala (Bordeaux), A.D. 310, and is believed to have had on the site of the present vineyard the villa wherein he wrote poems praising the wine of his native district and others.

Just as the French have borrowed from the British all their sporting terms, including the actual word "sport," the drinking customs of modern man—the drinking of healths, the touching of glasses, etc.— are borrowed from the ancients. And so are some of the most useful words in the modern terminology of the wine-lover and gourmet. When we speak of someone as a "sybarite," we liken him to an inhabitant of the Greek city of Sybaris, famous twenty-five centuries ago for luxurious living; when a small-town editor describes the Elks' banquet as a "Lucullan feast," his adjective has an ancestry that reaches back two thousand years to a cultured and self-indulgent Roman general; and when we call a man an epicure —which in these times, alas, we seldom can—we name him a spiritual descendant of the Greek philosopher Epicurus, who taught that pleasure is the only end of rational action, and uttered the wise warning: "Be moderate in all things that you may taste fully the joys of life."

∽ ∽

THE MIDDLE ERA

In medieval Europe minstrels sang of wine, and nobles, churchmen, men-at-arms, and peasants drank it. The early history of many of the great vineyards of France, including those of the Rhône Valley, Bordeaux, and the Côte d'Or, whence come the noblest Burgundies today, is bound up with ecclesiastical history. The rich Rhône wine called Châteauneuf-du-Pape was known in very early times, and its name ("new castle of the Pope") came through the fact that it grows where the popes had a summer palace in the fourteenth century, during the period of their residence at Avignon. The Bordeaux wine known as Château Pape Clément came from a vineyard said to have been planted for the wine-loving Pope Clement V, who was born either on the site of the present vineyard or near by. This was the same Pope Clement who moved the papal headquarters from Rome to Avignon in 1309.

Especially in the Côte d'Or the story of the vine is that of the church. Most of the greatest Burgundian vineyards known today belonged, long ago, to a few powerful monasteries, whose inmates, famous lovers of good living, developed their vineyards to the highest point then possible.

In his *A Book of French Wines,* which holds the place of honor on the shelves of many a student of the grape, P. Morton Shand relates some of this early history. In the year 630, he tells us, the Duke of Amalgaire gave the vineyard thenceforth to be known as the Clos de Bèze to the abbey of that name, which, in the thirteenth century, sold it to the abbey of Cluny—an abbey so powerful that it had been able to emerge victorious from quarrels with the dukes of Burgundy. At about the time of this sale a peasant named Bertin, who owned a strip of land adjoining the Clos de Bèze, planted a vineyard, which he tended with the same sedulous care as the monks displayed in tending theirs. This vineyard came to be known as the "field of Bertin," or *"champ de Bertin,"* which was ultimately contracted to Chambertin. Centuries later Chambertin was the favorite wine of Napoleon, and tradition tells us that he placed sufficient credence in Burgundian folklore to hope that Josephine, with the aid of generous drafts of Chambertin, could give him a male child.

Another very great red Burgundy, Clos de Tart, comes from a vineyard that was bought in the twelfth century by the nuns of Notre-Dame de Tart. Still another, Clos de Vougeot, is grown on land that was acquired in the early part of the fourteenth century by monks of the Cistercian order. It is related that an abbot of the old Cistercian monastery of Le Clos Vougeot sent the Pope some of his precious wine and was presently created Cardinal.

By a tradition dating from the time of the Napoleonic Wars, the vineyard of Clos de Vougeot is accorded military honors by French troops who pass that way. This custom, Stendhal tells us, originated with a certain Colonel Bisson who, marching with his regiment to join the Army of the Rhine, called a halt before the famous vineyard and brought his men to the salute. The idea was generally approved, and so it has lived on. Stendhal says that Colonel Bisson later became a general, and I think it fair to assume that this was the same General Bisson of whom Brillat-Savarin writes that he drank each day eight bottles of wine at his breakfast:

> He had a larger glass than the others, and emptied it oftener; but you would have said he did not care for it, for having thus imbibed sixteen pints of wine, he was as able to jest and give his orders as if he had only drunk a small decanter.

No one can write of food and wine without a thought for Master François Rabelais, wit, satirist, and glutton of sixteenth-century France. Born in Chinon, educated in a monastery, and himself a monk for many years, Rabelais early came to love the pleasures of the table. In his quieter moments he cultivated his own vineyard, La Devinière at Chinon, in which occupation he combined appreciation with real knowledge. It is not for his quiet moments that Rabelais is celebrated, however, and his robustious bellowings about food and drink make one think of him as a French Falstaff, which perhaps he was.

For Shakespeare was born only a few years after the death of Rabelais, and a few years later still he created Falstaff, whose panegyric to "Sherris-Sack" savors strongly of Pantagruel and is the delight of hearty drinking men:

> . . . Good faith, this same young sober-blooded boy doth not love me; nor a man cannot make him laugh;

but that's no marvel, he drinks no wine. There's never none of these demure boys come to any proof; for thin drink doth so over-cool their blood, and making many fish-meals, that they fall into a kind of male greensickness; and then, when they marry, they get wenches; they are generally fools and cowards; which some of us should be too, but for inflammation. A good sherris-sack hath a twofold operation in it. It ascends me into the brain; dries me there all the foolish and dull and crudy vapours which environ it; makes it apprehensive, quick, forgetive, full of nimble fiery and delectable shapes; which, delivered o'er to the voice, the tongue, which is the birth, becomes excellent wit. The second property of your excellent sherris is the warming of the blood; which, before cold and settled, left the liver white and pale, which is the badge of pusillanimity and cowardice; but the sherris warms it and makes it course from the inwards to the parts extreme. . . .

Falstaff's "Sherris-Sack" was nothing more or less than the crude ancestor of the strong Spanish wine more lately known as Sherry, and the words "Sherris" and "Sherry" represent efforts to anglicize the name of the Spanish town from which the wine comes: Jerez (or, as the old spelling had it, Xeres) de la Frontera. "Sack" we can suppose to be derived from the Spanish word *seco*, meaning dry.

Sack became popular in England in the sixteenth century, and thenceforward its pleasant fragrance permeates English literature. Thus, under date of

24 August 1660 we find Samuel Pepys writing in his Diary:

> Hence to Whitehall to the Privy Seal, but nothing to do. At night by land to my father's, where I found my mother not very well. I did give her a pint of sack.

Whether the Sack fed by Pepys to his mother was Sherry-Sack or some other sort of Sack we do not know; for just as, with the Dutch, the term "Schnapps" generally, but not always, meant gin, so in Pepys's day, and earlier, the term "Sack" seems generally to have meant Sherry, but sometimes to have referred to other heavy wines, such as Palma, Teneriffe, Canary, or Madeira.

Not only Sack but other ancient names of various wines emerge from the literature of the middle era. One finds reference to Gascon wine, or it may be Rhenish, Malvoisie, or Malmsey.

Gascon wine is the old name for the wine of Bordeaux. Rhenish was the ancestor of what we call Rhine wine and the English call Hock—a stupid appellation somehow devised from Hochheimer, the name of one of the many Rhine wines. Malvoisie I seem to remember as a wine introduced by the historical romancers in their more tender scenes—a wine that might be lightly sipped by the beautiful and mysterious lady at the inn. Beautiful and mysterious ladies of our time will perhaps be interested to know that this wine is still produced on the island of Lipari, where the ill-fated Mussolini sent his political prisoners, and that it is listed on Italian wine-cards as Malvasia.

Malvasia, it appears, was grown originally by the Greeks and found its way somehow, long ago, to the Canary Islands and Madeira. When the British began to drink it they changed its name, as is their way with wines. They called it Malmsey, and those who have not forgotten their English history will recall that George Plantagenet, Duke of Clarence, murdered in 1487, is said to have been drowned in a butt of Malmsey—which reminds me that the word "butt" meaning a cask (or, as it is called in the Madeira trade, a "pipe"), derives from "boot," which was the ancient name for a leathern wine-container. These containers, made from oxhides, sometimes held as much as sixty gallons. Smaller ones made from goatskins or kidskins, and smeared with pitch on the inside, were in common use in Biblical times, and when the Lord, in a parable, stated that "no man putteth new wine into old bottles . . ." He was speaking to people who made and stored their wine in leathern containers and illustrating by the fact, plainly understood by all who listened, that new wine could not safely be put into a vessel hopelessly impregnated with the fermentation of a former year.

Let come what may, the British stick to their traditions. They stick to tradition as they do to old stage favorites—it's a nice kind of loyalty. Thus the wines of modern England are Claret, Hock, Sherry,

Port, Champagne, and some Madeira; and a good deal of English history is written in these wines.

Claret became known to the English in the twelfth century. It arrived as the result of the marriage of Henry Plantagenet, later King Henry II, to Eleanor of Aquitaine. By this marriage the ancient province of Gascony, in which Bordeaux is situated, came under the dominion of the British Crown, and so remained for three hundred years, enabling Gascon wine-merchants to trade in England on favorable terms. In those days, apparently, the region immediately about Bordeaux produced wines that were thin and acid and did not travel well; the best wines came from the back country, up the River Garonne, and it is amusing, now, to read of the agelong struggles of the British to obtain the better wines, and of the obstructions put in their way by the Bordelais wine-merchants, who wished to dispose of their own thin wines and keep the better ones for home consumption or for blending-purposes.

French obstinacy was in this situation equal to British tenacity, and after some centuries of bickering, the English began to buy their wines, both French and German, at Antwerp, Amsterdam, and Rotterdam, where they were better treated, and Bordeaux, through cussedness, ceased to be the world's chief wine port.

The record of the Rhine as a wine-growing region dates back to the second century, and German wines were drunk in Britain as early as the tenth century.

When British trade removed from Bordeaux to the Dutch ports, the use of these wines in England increased, but the taste for *"clairet"* had been formed, and nothing has ever displaced it; Claret was Queen Victoria's favorite wine, and every good British wine-list is strong in this department. It is in Burgundies and Rhônes that the British are notoriously weak. Rhône wines were not included in the 1946 wine chart made by M. André Simon, distinguished British writer on wine and gastronomy.

The introduction of Sherry into England in the sixteenth century resulted not from popular demand but from England's quarreling with France and her efforts to seek favor with Spain. Sherry-Sack was an immense success, and now, after more than four centuries, the British are still drinking it.

Port wine, too, was first imported into England for political reasons. The eighteenth century found Queen Anne at loggerheads with Louis XIV, and, wishing to damage France, she struck at the wine trade, taxing French wine eight times the rate paid by the wine of Portugal. And so, along with their beloved Claret, Hock, Sherry, and the Madeira their officers learned to like while serving in America during the French and Indian Wars and the War of the Revolution, the good old steady-going British still drink Port.

∽ ∽

AMERICAN DRINKING HABITS

Like American common law and old-style American cooking, American drinking habits are an inheritance from Britain, plus a few local trimmings, not all of which are good.

The hardy men who first settled New England met a winter climate even more severe than that of their native land. Their life was not the life of luxury that goes with the drinking of fine wines, but one of hard physical exertion; wherefore drinking was with them a practical rather than an æsthetic matter. They drank to keep warm, to fortify themselves against fatigue, and to bolster flagging spirits. Rum and Brandy were their principal drinks, hot buttered Rum being the big favorite in New England inns from the beginning. In the region of Manhattan Island, where the Dutch had settled, the drink was Schnapps.

As we began to mold ourselves into a nation, some of our inhabitants took to the sea, like their British forebears, while others pressed into the wilderness. The pioneer, traveling afoot, on horseback, or in a canoe, had to travel light. The liquor that was a part of his baggage was in concentrated form: high-proof spirits that could stand a lot of dilution, and, fortunately for the Indian he met, the fire-water that he used for barter was oftentimes more water than fire.

Gradually a certain ease and elegance found their

way into American life, and the heavy wines popular
in England began to be drunk by gentlemen over
here. Madeira was in the greatest demand. In *The
Flowering of New England*, Van Wyck Brooks credits
Madeira with having been a principal solvent for the
grim puritanism of that region, and points out that
the society of New England seaport cities was hu-
manized long before that of inland cities because
Madeira wines reached the seaports first. What was
true for coastal New England was true elsewhere,
the ports of the South having a Madeira tradition as
long and as brilliant as any New York and New
England can claim.

Aside from the obviously superior quality of the
wine, various theories are advanced as to why Madeira became such an institution in late colonial and
early federal America, one of the most plausible and
defensible being a conclusion reached by a Boston
friend after studying family letters: the drinking
water on the Madeira Islands was so much better
than the water to be found in Spain that American
ships regularly put in at the islands to fill their water
butts, and pipes of Madeira were carried away.

Throughout our early days, moreover, many good
men, some of them highly influential, tried in every
way to foster wine-making and wine-drinking. William Penn made wine in his own vineyard, and early
in the seventeenth century Lord Delaware imported
cuttings of the best European vines and skilled
French viticulturists to tend them. Thomas Jefferson,

who advocated the drinking of wine, interested himself in the importation of vines and the planting of vineyards. All efforts to keep the vines alive and bearing failed. They liked neither the climate nor the pests they met and in a short time sickened and died. The colonists, who had a vision of building up an export wine industry comparable with the tobacco industry, did not give up, however, and attempts to establish vineyards were made along the seaboard from New England to Georgia. In Louisiana the French were trying the same thing, while in distant California, the Spanish padres were making their own wines from Mission grapes.

Almost all of these experiments were based on the theory that since this continent produced wild grapes in greater profusion than any other, European grapes should be made to flourish here, and for a long time no attention was paid to the native vine. In the early part of the last century, however, experiments undertaken in the eastern portion of the country in the cross-breeding and domestication of native American grapes were proving successful, and by 1850 there were prosperous vineyards in the Ohio River valley, central New Jersey, the Hudson River valley, the Finger Lakes region of New York State, on the south shore of Lake Erie, in the Carolinas, in Missouri, and in Michigan.

At about this time the California wine industry began in earnest, commercial growers taking over from the faltering missions. The first grower of any consequence to resume the effort to make European vines thrive on this continent was Jean Louis Vignes. Vignes was followed by a greater gambler in the field, Count Ágoston Haraszthy, who arrived in California in 1849 and by 1858 had a large vineyard in Sonoma County planted with imported vines. Haraszthy, full of Magyar enthusiasm, did a great deal to encourage vine-growing, and though his own venture was a failure, his was the stimulus that started the industry on its way, and California now produces more than eighty-five per cent of all wines made in the United States.

There are those who say Americans are not wine-drinkers and that nothing will change them.

Against this hard generalization are a few hopeful facts, chief among them being that the consumption of wine in this country is on the increase. True, the increase has not been as great as was expected at the time of Repeal; why we looked so confidently to a sudden renaissance of civilized drinking and appreciation, it is difficult now to say. Save in cities large enough to boast a traveled population and splendid dining-places, wine was almost unknown before Prohibition. Actually the annual consumption of wine in this country before that event averaged about half a gallon per person, as against about thirty gallons in France and Italy. During the Prohibition era a whole generation came to maturity knowing nothing about wine and caring for nothing in the way of drink but raw whisky and the gin they made in their own bathtubs and aged for fifteen minutes.

In addition, the interest in wine immediately after Repeal was not a healthy one. Wine was a novelty, something new to play with, and the impetus was toward the fashionable thing to do rather than to a resumption of the normal. We were witnessing high and temporary excitement rather than true interest.

Gradually this situation has been righting itself. Wine is still not that good familiar creature to us, but we are making headway at becoming acquainted. Partly this has resulted from the good wines which, except for unavoidable breaks in the pattern, have been coming into this country from abroad, many of them retailed at prices so reasonable as to make it impossible to dismiss wine as merely the toy of millionaires.

And partly it is a natural outcome of the strides the American industry has made, progressing from its almost humiliatingly bad start directly after Repeal to its present production of gallons numbered in the dozens of millions. As with the other wine regions of the world, only a small portion of this harvest can be considered wine of quality, but certain of the California growers are not only expanding output but are endeavoring at the same time to improve their product; and in the wineries of the Eastern states the efforts to arrive at wine of distinction never ceases. Here and there in both sections of the country individuals of tremendous idealism are working with assurance and devotion; and if it be true that much indifferent wine finds its way to the market, it is equally true that occasionally one can raise a glass in toast to a really fine one.

It takes time for the taste of a people to change, let alone be educated—time and sufficient exposure to the new idea. We began as a nation of hard-liquor drinkers, we continued up to Prohibition as a nation of hard-liquor drinkers, and during Prohibition we gave free rein to the perversity that is one of our national traits, treated the law as a challenge, and drank hard liquor with two hands instead of one. It may still be true that we cannot be made into wine-drinkers, but signs and portents, and yearly statistics each more impressive than the last, seem to indicate a broadening appreciation of the place wine occupies in the pattern of good living.

CHAPTER TWO

A BROAD LOOK AT WINES

I think wealth has lost much of its value if it have not wine. I abstain from wine only on account of the expense. When I heard that Mr. Sturgis had given up wine, I had the same regret that I had lately in hearing that Mr. Bowditch had broken his hip. . . .

—RALPH WALDO EMERSON

Wine is the fermented juice of the grape, and the principal types of wine fall into four loose groupings:

(1) Natural still wines, which vary from dry to sweet and are generally understood to be made from the fermented juice of grapes grown in a specified vineyard in a specified year; (2) blended wines, which may be still, sparkling, or fortified, and are made from grapes that may or may not have been grown in the same vineyard or even in the same year; (3) fortified wines, which are made from the fermented juice of the grape to which has been added at a decisive stage in its fermentation a quantity of a spirit especially distilled from wine; (4) sparkling wines, either natural or artificial, the latter made by

the addition of syrup, again at the proper moment, to induce a second fermentation. To the above should be added brandies, which are distilled from wine.

Excepting certain special wines, such as Sherry, Madeira, Port, and Tokay, wines are generally spoken of as being either red or white; but the actual shade of a white wine may run all the way from pale straw-color to deep amber, and the depth and subtlety of coloring in red wine varies greatly. In between the red and the white wines are the pinks, or *rosés*. Contrary to supposition, red wines are not always made from red grapes and white wines from white grapes. In the making of Champagne, for instance, deep purple and white grapes are used together in proportions varying according to the blend. Red wines are made, and are given their color, by allowing the juice to ferment for a time in contact with the skins, pips, and sometimes even the stems; white wines by fermenting the clear juice. In the making of *rosé* wines, the juice is fermented for a short period in contact with the skins, and then drawn off. *Rosé* wines are made also by blending red and white wines, with the white predominating, but such artifice seldom makes a good wine.

France is the supreme wine country of the world; her wines are more abundant and, at their greatest, better than those of other lands. Even the secondary wines of France frequently surpass most wines of other countries. Next in merit to French wines are those of Germany. Nearly all German wines are white and there is less variety among them than among French wines. While the top ones are magnificent and costly in great vintage years, they are very often sweet, with a kind of sweetness that makes it difficult to fit them properly into meals.

Second to France in volume of production and in variety comes Italy. Italian wines are at their best extremely pleasing, but compared with French wines, they are coarse. Spain exports a number of wines, but is known to us principally for Sherry, though Spanish Brandies are worth looking into, being next in excellence to the best French Brandies. Hungary makes Tokay and other varieties; Portugal, Port, Brandy, and unpretentious natural wines slightly on the sweet side; from Switzerland comes Neuchâtel and other excellent white wines; and the product of the Madeira Islands is well known. Wines of many kinds are grown in French North Africa, in South Africa, and in Australia, and much more wine is grown in South America than in North America. The ascendancy of France is so complete, however, that the study of wines always begins and often ends there.

France produces natural still red wines, natural still white wines, some blended wines in both colors, a few pinks, which are exported in limited quantities and when shipped generally lose all the quality that makes them most agreeable at home, and sparkling wines, both natural and manufactured. Her most famous wines come from six regions: Champagne, Bordeaux, Burgundy, the valley of the Rhône, the valley of the Loire, and Alsace-Lorraine. The wines of each district show a definite family resemblance, and this likeness within the group is not limited to the wines of France. It is characteristic in all of the major wine-growing districts of the world where the wines are not tampered with to such an extent that the inherent grape flavor is lost.

The essentials of wine-making are simple. In the early autumn, before the grapes are picked, they show on the surface of the skin a misty coating, known in the trade as the "bloom." The bloom is actually a mass of minute living organisms, which, immediately the grapes are pressed, begin feeding on the natural grape sugar in the juice, transforming the sugar into alcohol and discharging carbonic-acid gas into the air. The organic process by which this change takes place is called fermentation. When fermentation stops, the new wine is drawn off into clean casks, generally made of oak, which are kept filled to the bung to prevent harmful bacteria from reaching the wine and turning it into vinegar or worse. Now begins the period of maturing in the wood, the interval during which the wine responds to careful handling while it throws off its greatest volume of grape solids, gradually loses its initial hardness, and develops to the right point for bottling.

In the great wine regions of France generations of wine-growers, following one upon the other through the ages, have built up what is practically a special race, rich in experience and skill. Each has proved the worth of a method of wine-making for a particular grape variety grown on a particular piece of soil, and they understand their wines better than they understand their wives. Yet even these hereditary experts cannot predict with certainty what character their wine will take in any given year. With the weather favorable and all conditions seemingly at their best, they still cannot be certain. Even after the wine has been bottled and put to bed in the cellar to age, it may undergo changes, sudden and inexplicable.

For wine is a living thing. That has not always been known, but it is true. Lying in its air-tight bottle in a cool, dark catacomb, it is not dead, but resembles, rather, a philosopher who has retired to a cave to meditate for the enrichment of his soul.

Sometimes the result is disappointing. A wine that at the outset shows every sign of greatness may prove precocious and mature too fast. Or again, where no remarkable early promise has been shown, the wine may surprise the experts by developing unexpected qualities of distinction and longevity, forcing a revision of opinion concerning the merit of a certain year. Among great wines, those which at first taste rather coarse, and which seem reluctant to mature, often turn out best. They are worth waiting for. A poor year for one type of wine will sometimes be a good year for another type. Often it happens that the wine of one vineyard will be good when that of a neighboring vineyard is poor. This may result from the judgment used as to the time for harvesting the grapes, from permitting the juice to ferment on the skins for too long a time and thus acquiring an excess of tannin, from localized rain or hailstorms just before the harvest, or from one of several other causes.

Like human beings, wines sometimes become "sick" without apparent reason; while they are sick, their flavor is impaired; then they get well again. This happens to fairly young wines as well as to old ones. In the spring of 1945 I had an experience with an ailing wine that seems worth recounting. Home again after seven months away, I thought to celebrate our first lunch with a bottle of Claret, but it didn't turn out to be much of a celebration. The first bottle I brought from the cellar was the non-vintage Saint Emilion already mentioned, a modest district wine of which I had long been fond. I drew the cork, sniffed it, and was repelled by its musty, fungus odor. The wine had the same musty smell, and tasted hard and unpleasant.

I went for another bottle and this time produced a nobleman: Château Mouton-Rothschild 1929. Again the fungus smell and taste and the hard unpalatable wine. Alarmed lest disaster had befallen my whole cellar, I began an anxious tasting of all my favorite clarets, château-bottled wines of 1920, 1924, 1926, and so on up to 1934. All were good except another bottle of Mouton-Rothschild 1929, which exhibited the same defects as the earlier bottle. On this wine I tried an experiment. I brought it to the dining-room three hours before dinner, opened it, and let it stand uncorked in its cradle on the sideboard until we sat down to eat. By the time I poured it, it was much improved, and when I had rolled it in my glass for fifteen or twenty minutes, giving it a further chance to "breathe," its mustiness and hardness disappeared and it became a wine of the most exquisite delicacy and fragrance. With the passing months the initial hardness on opening diminished, and within six months the wine was entirely well again.

One of the Frenchest qualities about French wines is the dislike that many of them have for travel. The red wines, even more than the whites, become seasick or trainsick and must lie down and rest for a considerable time to recover from a journey. Most white wines, especially young ones, stand travel better than the more robust-appearing reds. At one time it was thought that certain delicate Vouvrays from Touraine and Saumurs from Anjou were the conspicuous exceptions to this rule. It was authoritatively held that these wines so like charming, temperamental women, turning suddenly, inexplicably, from grave to gay and back again, would not travel. This dictum has been disproved steadily in the intervening years, when they have come into this country in quantity and kept well, provided they have been good in the first place.

Wines that are fairly high in alcoholic content usually travel best, and people are often surprised to learn that, broadly speaking, white wines are slightly stronger in alcohol than reds, for the rich color of red wine somehow suggests that the opposite should be true.

It is the fate of Champagne to live merrily and die young. Champagne at fifteen years of age is well along in life, and at twenty it is likely to be dead. A fine Burgundy or Bordeaux of a great year, on the other hand, may live to a ripe old age if properly cared for. I have tasted some of the great pre-phylloxera wines of both these types which at the age of sixty years and older were superb. A wine as old as they will often have lost a great part of its potency, but it will have gained marvelously in suavity and bouquet, and to savor it is an experience.

Unfortunately we see few very old wines in this country. Besides being costly because of rarity, an ancient wine is extremely delicate; to ship a wine twenty or twenty-five years old is to subject it to great danger. The planting of new roots in most European vineyards to combat the pest phylloxera had, in the opinion of many experts, a damaging effect upon the wines. This pest, a root louse, was brought into France on American grape plants. The roots of American vines had built up a partial immunity to the louse, but the tender and unsuspecting roots of the European vine had no protection, and for a time it looked as if the destruction of the European vineyards might be complete. As we brought the illness, so we brought the cure. European vines were grafted onto American roots, and the vineyards were replanted. Since that time the constant argument, with very little agreement except on one side, has been over the merits of pre- versus post-phylloxera wines. As many of the arguers and most of the wines have disappeared, the noise has subsided, but it seems generally to be conceded that even the greatest wines of later years will not attain such ripe old age as did the noble elders of '64, '68, '69, '70, '74, '75, and '78, which were still being drunk with pleasure in the late 1930's. Wines now mature more rapidly and pass their "point" much earlier.

This is not altogether the disaster it would seem, for the hurried, crowded conditions of modern life are unfavorable to the laying down of wines against the distant future. A good wine-cellar, as George Meredith somewhere said, suggests a spacious solid house pervaded by a sense of permanency and well-being, and a family with roots in the ground. Life is not like that any more, and everything is against the long-time storage of wine: modern heating arrangements, the negligence of architects, themselves the followers of an art, in making proper provision for wine storage when designing houses, and the crowded city apartments where space is wanting and temperatures are hostile. The average person purchasing wines today is likely to look only a year or two ahead, and a cellar planned with a thought for five or ten years hence will be exceptional. The old rooted feeling has disappeared.

The study of wines resembles in one respect the study of history; each study leads the mind upon a dual course, entertaining it with legends odd and romantic, but compelling it to master names and dates.

The principle has often been laid down that a good name must be in conjunction with a good year to produce a satisfactory wine. By this is meant a wine of good reputation bottled by the grower, according to the excellent custom practiced in Bordeaux and in other wine districts where the standard of quality is high; or a wine of good reputation which, if not bottled by the grower, has behind it the name of an honest shipper.

The principle is sound but limiting. It does not entirely rule out the arts of the blender, but it does rule out the many good names that are not widely known. In fine years humble vineyards will sometimes catch up the song of their great neighbors and sing it so well that for a season they are almost prima donnas, though not at prima donnas' pay. A relatively humble wine of a great year will surpass a famous wine of a poor year, yet will sell at a low price.

As to names, it is an amusing fact that wines having names which Americans and Englishmen find it easy to pronounce sell at higher prices than certain other meritorious wines the names of which embarrass alien tongues. It happens that such names as Ausone, Latour, Yquem, and Chambertin, all belonging to great wines, trip lightly from our lips, and in a special category is the easily remembered Pontet-Canet, a Fifth-Cru Médoc, which was prominently displayed on all wine-lists in this country for many years; but we seldom see on export lists such names as Ducru-Beaucaillou, Malescot-Saint-Exupéry, or Clerc-Milon-Mondon, good Clarets all; nor Suduiraut or Rayne-Vigneau, so close in merit to the great Yquem; nor yet Grands Éschézeaux, which comes not far behind the noble Chambertin. All these are less expensive than the wines first mentioned, and the difference in price is in many cases greater than the difference in merit.

To buy pleasant wines at reasonable prices, the study of wine classifications and vintage years is important, as is some knowledge of the laws and regulations governing wine in each country; a spirit of adventure also is necessary and perhaps the most valuable of all is a connection with a reliable and wine-wise dealer.

Our ignorance of all matters pertaining to wine has cost us dear. Much of the low-grade wine Americans are offered by their own industry would disappear if the buying public developed sufficient knowledge to be critical. And abroad we have always been considered fair game, particularly by the French. There is a certain type of American who, when in doubt, thinks to protect himself by ordering an expensive wine.

A friend of mine, motoring on a main French highway, stopped at a pleasant inn for luncheon, and upon looking at the wine-list was surprised to discover that wines of poor years were priced higher than those of good years.

"What is the reason for this?" he asked the proprietor.

"It is simple, monsieur," replied the other. "Many American motorists stop here, and Americans know nothing of wines. Always they order the most costly. By marking up the prices of our poor wines we sell them profitably to strangers and at the same time save our best wines for our regular clients."

The story points its own moral, and that moral is important not only to the American consumer abroad but to the American buyer at home. As in all enterprises having to do with growth and change, and at the mercy of the calculating in human nature, the ignorant consumer is given little heed, and only continued rejection of an inferior product will deter the eager wine-growers from shipping their poorest wines across the country, or over the seas.

Of the many wonderful things about wine, perhaps the most wonderful is the fact that a thing so fragile has survived at all. Unlike the growing of ordinary annual farm crops, the growing of wine takes years or even decades of continued, skillful, tranquil, and devoted effort; yet ever since the mists of legend began to congeal into recorded history, Europe's great wine regions have at intervals endured invasion, destruction, pillage, and plague.

The second World War brought all but plague. From France came stories of desperate measures undertaken to protect stocks of wine: niches were dug into cellar walls, filled with fine wines, and walled up; whole corridors in the great caves of Champagne were closed; special labels were printed, and watered wine and the wines of poor years were shipped out in place of the great wines ordered. Not all of the measures were successful, and many cellars and storage warehouses were looted or the stocks ruthlessly destroyed. In the midst of this chaos and hardship, the French wine people plodded on, achieving the miracles of maintaining their vineyards, pressing the grapes, and making new wine each autumn—quantity was sharply cut, but two of the war years produced good wines—and of withholding better than half the annual production and a substantial amount of their stocks of older wines. In Germany sizable stocks of wine survived, as did their vineyards; and one somehow feels that the vineyards of Italy are indestructible.

The war's end brought new rather than diminished trials. There were the problems of finding bottles, corks for the bottles, wood for wine cases, and nails, and of hunting means of transportation where little existed. There was also the problem of new laws and regulations, or the lack of them, in occupied areas; and of overcoming prejudices newly created or long remembered.

However, wine itself has shown a power of assertion stronger than all obstructions and delays, and it has been moving for many years now, along its accustomed ways.

CHAPTER THREE

THE WINES OF FRANCE

"They order," said I, "this matter better in France."
—LAURENCE STERNE
(*A Sentimental Journey*)

CHAMPAGNE

Champagne, most widely known of wines of the world round, is made in the region of Reims, Epernay, and Châlons-sur-Marne, in what was the ancient province of Champagne, and it stands in a class alone among sparkling wines. The sparkling-wine process is a complicated one, consisting in imprisoning in the bottle a portion of the carbonic acid gas that in a normal fermentation bubbles into the air and is lost; and because Champagne is elaborately treated before and during its life in bottle, it is often called a manufactured wine.

For the pressing, black and white grapes from the neighborhood vineyards of Champagne are used, the proportions a closely guarded secret of the wine houses. The wine is kept in casks until fermentation stops, and is "racked"—that is, drawn off its lees into clean casks—several times during this period. As soon as the new wine is clear, it is blended with wines of the same vintage, or in deficient years with older wines that add such qualities as it seems to need: strong wines if it be weak in alcohol; delicate wines if it be strong. In wine language this blend has come to be called the *cuvée*.

When the blend is made, the sugar content of the wine is analyzed, enough sugar in the form of syrup is added to induce a second fermentation, and the wine is bottled. The bottling takes place in the spring of the year following the harvest, and with corks fastened down by heavy clamps, the wine is laid away in cool subcellars for at least three years, to develop its sparkle and throw off whatever the second fermentation has produced in the way of solids. The bottles are then moved into special racks, tilted neck down at about a sixty-degree angle, and the sediment, by skillful handling, is coaxed to settle next the cork; the wine in the neck of the bottle is frozen, the cork is extracted, and with it comes the sediment which is held in the ice that clings to the cork. The bottle is capped immediately to prevent the escape of gas while the wine awaits the final step in its intricate making.

At this juncture the wine is dry, as the first dosage of sugar has been changed into alcohol and carbonic-acid gas, leaving no residue of sweetness. A second dosage is therefore given, this consisting of old wine in which cane sugar is dissolved, in amounts that vary according to the sweetness or dryness desired by the market to which the wine will go. (The word "dry" as applied to wine means the opposite of sweet, without, however, meaning sour.) Very fine Cognac Brandy is sometimes added to fortify the wine. The bottles are now recorked and again strongly wired, and they are ready for market. This entire operation, requiring hand work of the most expert kind and consuming four or five years, is one part of the reason why Champagne is so expensive. The other part is the high luxury tax levied against all sparkling wines, this tax, plus duty, amounting to more than eight times that charged against still wines.

In great vintage years the best Champagnes require little or no blending, and these years produce the dated or vintage wines. Non-vintage Champagnes can be very pleasant and in some cases astonishingly good, but they should be bought only when they have behind them the unquestioned reputation of a good house. I had far rather drink the light and pleasant Ackerman-Laurance, Dry Royal, grown on the hills of Saumur and made by the champagne process, than risk hard and acid non-vintage Champagnes of unknown brands, many of which are fit only for launching ships.

Champagne is generally at its best in from ten to fifteen years. It is supposed to last twenty years, and while I have drunk some beautiful old Champagnes

—in 1935 I tasted a Krug 1904, a Pol Roger 1904, and a Perrier-Jouët 1906, and each was superb—the chances are that by twenty years most wines will be fading and some bottles will have gone flat. The oldest Champagne I ever tasted was a Moët et Chandon, Vin de Champagne, Imperial 1874. This bottle, the gift of M. André Simon, was served at a dinner given in its honor in June of 1935. In the Moët et Chandon Cellars at Epernay, twenty-eight bottles were opened to get six good ones, the sediment was removed, and the bottles recorked. The label is enshrined on its own page in a cellar-book. The wine described on the one following: "This is undoubtedly the most remarkable Champagne any of us will ever drink. A superb, delicate, marvellously smooth wine in perfect condition—61 years old!"

The credit for the inspiration which finally produced Champagne must be given to the monk Dom Pérignon, of the Abbey of Hautvillers. His ordination as cellar-master coincided with efforts by the local wine-growers to breed out the natural sparkle which was typical of the wines of the district. Under his persuasive guidance the trend was reversed, and the long and complicated experiments to increase and hold the sparkle in bottle were begun. At the beginning of its history Champagne was an excessively sweet wine, and the French, who still drink rather sweet Champagne, consider it a dessert wine. Dry Champagne was first made to fill a demand from

England. This turned it from a dessert wine into what is probably the most useful of general service wines.

I never was deeply interested in Champagne, but I have become fond enough of it to agree that a very fine and very dry Champagne is one of the great triumphs of the arts of wine-growing and wine-making; nevertheless I still do not feel that it is the aristocrat of wines. There is no doubt that Champagne is a wine of many purposes. It is fresh and gay, unsurpassed for festive occasions and comforting and delightful at any hour of the day or evening, served with a wafer or without. But it lacks the ultimate refinement of great Clarets and the vigorous authority of great Burgundies, and when it is served throughout a dinner I am inclined to suspect the host of taking a lazy man's short cut to settling his wine problem. One cannot say that it is not correct, but it seems to me a little stupid.

The terms used to designate degrees of sweetness are as follows:

Brut ought to mean natural and should signify a wine unfortified, unsweetened, and even unblended, but it generally denotes "driest," meaning only that sugar and other extraneous matter have been kept down to a minimum. A *brut* Champagne may need as little as one half of one per cent of the second dosage, while a sweet Champagne may contain up to twelve and fifteen per cent, or over. *Sec* means dry, as against sweet, so of course *Extra Sec* means extra dry. *Demi-Sec* is supposed to mean middling dry;

Demi-Doux middling sweet, and *Doux* sweet. Wines labeled *Goût Américain* or *Drapeau Américain,* though marked *Sec,* are too often sweet wines destined for South America and need not concern us.

The American cult for "dry" which is really not dry at all, the little self-deception that makes so many of us "talk dry but sing sweet," is well understood in France and consequently the terms for dry are not always reliable. Many Champagnes marked *Extra Dry* are medium dry when tasted, and those marked *Dry* are often much too heavily dosed. Only practical tests will determine which designation is preferred and the experiments should begin with *Brut, Extra Sec,* and *Sec.* It is certain that for making a good dry Champagne the best wine must be used, whereas the failings of a poor wine may be concealed by sugar.

Probably the finest Champagne made is that produced by the important houses and marked "English Cuvée." A fair amount of wine thus labeled comes into this country, but it has been my experience that English Cuvée wines stamped ENGLAND or shipped via the English market are more delicate and have greater finesse and better balance than English Cuvée wines sent us direct from France. Other Cuvée markings are "Private," "Reserve," "Extra," and "Spéciale," all implying blends a cut above the ordinary.

Champagne should be served out of the largest possible bottle, the quality of the wine improving as the size of the bottle grows. Sweet or very old Champagnes need more icing than do dry, moderately young wines. A poor Champagne, or one that is too young or that is not adequately iced, is likely to open with a loud report and bubble over, but a good Champagne, properly iced, should open with a discreet sound and behave itself with dignity and decorum. A thin blue smoke should hover momentarily around the mouth of the bottle, and the wine when poured should show small bubbles rising lightly like a fine powder, and its gentle effervescence should endure for a long time. The shape of the glass has a good deal to do with the length of time a Champagne holds its sparkle. Champagne is best served in large glasses, the interior of the bowl descending at the base to the point which seems to encourage the bubbles. The most satisfactory glass is the Champagne flute, rather like a Sherry glass but larger. The small saucer glasses are an abomination we inherited from the Victorian age.

The storage of Champagne is important. Because of the imprisoned gas, corks tend to dry out sooner than with still wines. The bottles can lie tilted slightly toward the cork, or the necks of the bottles may be dipped in paraffin to keep the corks airtight.

There are a number of fine wine houses in Champagne, exporting brands long and favorably known. By the most skillful blending, each house manages to produce a precise flavor and to keep it fairly constant from year to year. The inexperienced buyer of

Champagne will do best for himself if he learns a few brands and vintage years which please him and, unless he is under expert guidance, keeps to the better-known names and the good years, remembering always that only a *very good* Champagne is noteworthy.

Some of the recommended houses are:

Krug, Veuve Clicquot, Lanson, Perrier-Jouët, Bollinger, Moët et Chandon, Pol Roger, Ruinart, Roederer, Irroy, Ayala, Delbeck, Mumm, Pommery & Greno, Piper-Heidsieck, Charles Heidsieck, and Goulet.

VINTAGE YEARS IN CHAMPAGNE

Good wines were made in the years 1942 and 1943, but, except for the isolated great ones still remaining, the wines of these years have become memories. The 1945's were very fine and the 1947's great, both years maturing early. 1949 produced splendid and longer-lived wines, and 1950 fairly good ones. Great wines were made in 1952 and 1953, 1952 being one of the best years in recent times. 1955 was a great year, 1957 a year of good wines but meager yield, and 1959 is mentioned in superlatives. The wines of the intervening years can be described, at the best, as fair.

∽ ∽

BORDEAUX WINES

RED BORDEAUX (CLARET)

When Louis XIV was ailing, the Duc de Richelieu urged him to drink red Bordeaux for his health, but the monarch flouted it as merely "a passable little wine." Dr. Johnson, in his much quoted epigram: "Claret for boys, port for men; but he who aspires to be a hero must drink brandy," also spoke slightlyingly of Claret. But such disparagements of a great wine reflect only upon the taste of those who utter them. Bordeaux wines are among the world's greatest, and they were great long before good Samuel Pepys drank what he called "Ho-Bryen"—otherwise Haut-Brion.

The wine region of Bordeaux is officially limited to the Department of the Gironde, and no wines grown outside that department may legally be designated as Bordeaux. Within the department about fifteen per cent of the acreage is devoted to the growing of the vine, and the region offers a great variety of production. Because of the excellent manner in which the Bordeaux trade is regulated, and the classification of the principal Bordeaux wines, these are perhaps the safest wines from the point of view of the purchaser. One needs little special knowledge to get an excellent Bordeaux.

The principal red wines of Bordeaux come from four districts: Médoc, Graves, Saint Emilion, and

Pomerol. In Graves white wines are produced in slightly smaller quantity than red wines. No white wine of any great consequence is produced in the other three districts.

Between disciples of red Bordeaux and red Burgundy, the two great wines of France, there has long raged a controversy as to which is the greater, but the controversy can never be settled because it is entirely a question of taste. Burgundy-lovers maintain that a fine red Burgundy is a noble thing, like matchless music or painting, and that it is more robust and commanding than any Bordeaux, however distinguished; but the champions of Bordeaux mention certain Moutons and Latours and Ausones and contend that their beloved wine excels in delicacy and complexity, and is therefore entitled to first rank. At all events, Burgundy is often called the King of Wines and Bordeaux the Queen, and these titles do in fact suggest the nature of the difference between them. A red Burgundy of a great year, properly matured, must always take the place of honor over other wines. In its gorgeous ruby robe it enters at the supreme moment of the repast, regal, self-confident, a trifle swaggering, aware that nothing can surpass it. A red Bordeaux of equal merit in its kind is like a sensitive and lovely woman, a true aristocrat, who neither vaunts her charms nor too modestly conceals them. Their very bottles seem to indicate their qualities: hers, straight and slender, with shoulders carried proudly high; his, jovial and thick-bodied, with a rotundity suggesting a good paunch. The Belgian Burgundy bottle is lower and stouter still.

The lamentable truth is that the swaggering Burgundian is sometimes a good deal of a rascal, whereas, if you understand the lady of Bordeaux a little, you can trust her. And that understanding is important to Americans. Just as the climatic conditions of Belgium bring out the best in Burgundy, making that wine not only the most suitable but also the favorite wine of the country, so the climate of our country seems especially favorable for the maturing of Clarets. We have as good Clarets as are available in any country outside France.

The greater integrity of Bordeaux wines arises from two facts. First, the leading wines of the region are officially classified in groups (*crus,* or growths), giving each wine of consequence a rating; and second, the majority of the best Bordeaux wine-growers bottle at least a part, and often all, of their own wines, and label the bottles with their distinctive château labels.

In Médoc, the district producing almost all the finest red Bordeaux, the sixty classed growths divided into five groups stand at the top, like a viticultural royal family and peerage. In bad years most of the proprietors sell their wine in bulk to wholesalers with the stipulation that the latter, in reselling, cannot use the château name. In better years wholesalers who buy château wine are often permitted to use the château name upon their labels, backing it up with their own firm names. But the guarantee of a wholesaler is not generally considered as valuable as that of the estate or vineyard on which the wine was grown, and discriminating buyers are usually willing to pay a slightly higher price for château-bottled wine.

It is the custom of château proprietors who have bottled their own wines to state the fact explicitly upon their labels, usually with the words *Mis en bouteilles au Château, Mise du Château,* or the initials *M.D.C.* Further safeguard is afforded by the stamping of corks with one of the above-mentioned forms of assurance, together with the name of the château and the vintage year. Look at your corks. They can tell you a great deal. Learn to distinguish a springy new cork from an old one and to see how far the color of the wine runs up into the cork, another indication of age. The color on the bottom of a cork should be even and solid, not streaky.

In addition to the classified growths of the Médoc, there are many wines similarly treated but not judged worthy of classification: the *Crus Bourgeois Supérieur, Bourgeois, Artisans,* and *Paysans.* Hundreds of wines are listed in these groups, each with a vineyard name and generally carrying the mark of château-bottling and the proper *cru* designation. They come from every district of Bordeaux and account for about three quarters of the wine made each year. In most cases the wine is grown on soil not favorable for the production of fine wines, but when it is made with thought for quality it can transcend its humble origin and be surprisingly good.

Next in order comes the large group known as district or regional wines, labeled with the names of the communes or parishes where they are made: Margaux, Saint Julien, Saint Estèphe, Saint Emilion, Pomerol, and Graves. Many vineyard-owners raise grapes and make wine with no expectation of bottling or marketing their product. The wines are sold to merchants or shippers who journey through the districts, sampling from the cask, and completing the task of readying the wines for market at their warehouses. The wines are not remarkable, but a well-balanced cellar will contain a share of them. They are the stand-bys for family dining, and to give to friends whose bland admission rules out special interest in wine. The label of a district wine has the merit of claiming little, and the consumer must do his own research in this field. My choice long ago settled on the Saint Emilions. They are less astringent than the Saint Juliens, and seem more to be relied upon than wines in the same class made in the other communes.

A man who is trustworthy will tell you all about himself and so, in the vast majority of cases, will a wine. The label is the wine's business card, and the buyer in years past was warned away from such unrevealing and broadly generic designations as Bordeaux or Claret or Médoc. The labels not only told little, but, unless the shipper or importer was known to be reliable, that little was suspect. Recently the more responsible shippers of Bordeaux have taken this questionable situation in hand. A committee has been empowered not only to set a standard of quality but to taste-test wines in this class and price range which are destined for export. Wines which pass this keen scrutiny bear a black-and-gold seal stamped on the capsule or affixed to the neck of the bottle, the signature *Qualité Approuvée par ADEB*. The initials are unduly small, but they stand as safeguard against minor frauds and great, such as bottles labeled Bordeaux and shipped presumably from that port, which, when opened, display the surprising flavor of the Concord grape.

MÉDOC

Fifty-nine of the sixty classed *crus* of red Bordeaux come from Médoc, the odd one, Château Haut-Brion, being a Graves. The classification, which dates from 1855, is known as the Médoc Classification, and Château Haut-Brion was for convenience included as a Médoc. This classification has long been considered obsolete, and it is gratifying to learn that a start has been made on a new. The final result, dependent upon that elusive thing, concord, may be some time in reaching us, but it will be the voice of authority leading into a new era. Among the changes expected is the upgrading of Château Mouton-Rothschild. Four wines are listed in the *Premier* (First) *Cru:* Châteaux Lafite-Rothschild, Latour, Margaux, and Haut-Brion, which at their finest and most fragrant merit a special position. However, while the *premier cru* standard of Margaux and Haut-Brion was in question for a period of years, there has been no disputing the steady rise in quality of Château Mouton-Rothschild, in good years the equal in elegance of its peers.

Any of the sixty classified château wines, given a favorable year, should be more than ordinarily good and many should be great. The wines vary from commune to commune, and even within single vineyards, and each has its own individual flavor. The variation is not surprising when one considers the many factors that influence the character of a wine: the location of a vineyard, the quality of the soil, the amount of sun and air the plants receive, and the differences in vine-plants and methods of cultivation and wine-making. Nevertheless, all of the wines have much in common: their color, clear and brilliant, ruby rather than garnet, and the family flavor, frank, unmistakable, and infinitely pleasing.

There are good names in all *crus*. In the Second *Cru,* Château Gruaud-Larose has been consistently a good wine, and the same may be said of Rausan-Ségla and Cos d'Estournel. The latter is a "reluctant" wine, needing more age than most Médocs. Léoville-Las Cases in the Second *Cru* is a nice wine, full and rather aromatic, and Pichon-Longueville is a fine Claret with bouquet, breed, and all the rest of it. Château Cantenac-Brown in the Third *Cru* resembles Mouton-Rothschild in successful years and is a lovely big Claret; Château Palmer has the typical Margaux character, and La Lagune is a delightful luncheon Claret, quite light and refreshing, which in great years can be a great wine. Château Beychevelle in the Fourth *Cru* has the mellowness of all good Saint Juliens, and another excellent wine in this *cru* is Château Branaire-Ducru. The Rothschilds are making a fine wine out of Mouton d'Armailhacq, a Fifth *Cru* wine, and Pontet-Canet, also of the Fifth *Cru,* has always been popular in this country.

A word about the 1855 Médoc Classification: It should not be supposed that *cru* means class precisely or that Fifth *Cru* means a wine that is only one fifth as good as a First *Cru* wine. In good years and also in years when the weather is so uneven as to make it impossible to cling to exact listings, some wines of the Third, Fourth, and Fifth *Crus* partake of the characteristics of those at the top and win places of high distinction for themselves. The classification represents the cream of the Médoc production, and except for the rating of some few vineyards whose quality of production automatically places them in another class, and those whose wines now justify proper recognition, the old listing can be considered to be useful still.

RED GRAVES

Rabelais in the sixteenth century called Graves wines "gallant and fluttering." The district is famous for its white wines; nevertheless it produces more red wine than white, and finer red wines than white wines. Its celebrated Château Haut-Brion, the nearest of the great vineyards to the city of Bordeaux, used to be rated supreme, and surely at its peak the appellation "Roi des Graves" was amply justified. However, there are downs as well as ups in this business, and the wines made at Haut-Brion in the '20's and '30's were seldom of top quality. Since the war the vineyard has reclaimed a good part of its lost reputation, but in the unfortunate interval several of the first growths of the district began pushing it for top place. Château La Mission-Haut-Brion and Domaine de Chevalier are splendid wines, sometimes seeming even better than Haut-Brion; and Château Haut-Bailly is another deservedly well-known growth of Graves.

The wines from this district are apt to be hard when young—"green" is the word most often heard; and they need rather more aging to reveal their sweet fruitiness than those of the Médoc.

SAINT EMILION

The district of Saint Emilion grows straightforward red wines with such great intensity of flavor and bouquet that they are generally spoken of as being more full-bodied and robust than the Médocs and Graves—qualities which also have caused them to be called the Burgundies of Bordeaux. They are masculine wines, actually, only slightly less distinguished than the more delicate Médocs; and although usually shorter-lived than the Médocs, they can have a hard edge when young that only age can soften. Château Ausone was long given pre-eminence in this district, but in recent years Château Cheval Blanc has developed handsomely and is crowding hard to assume first place. Saint Emilion and its neighbor Pomerol suffered greatly in the frost of 1956, which destroyed many vines in both communes. Some years must elapse before these wines regain their old authority.

POMEROL

The wines of Pomerol are as a rule lighter than the Saint Emilions, smooth and often delicious, approaching in finesse the wines of the Médoc. They age in bottle more rapidly than the Médocs, and may be described as forward wines, showing an attractive flowery quality which invites early drinking. However, there are the inevitable exceptions: A Château Pétrus of 1929, the more precocious of the great twins, 1928 and 1929, fulfilled all hopes for it when opened twenty-five years later; yet it carried its age with such grace and strength that I felt it might easily have continued on for another decade.

Other widely known wines of this district are Château L'Evangile, Vieux Château Certan, and Château La Conseillante.

THE OLD ORDER CHANGETH

Marked alterations in vinification procedures have taken place in Europe in the last fifteen years.

The impetus to change was undoubtedly the fact that very small stocks of matured wine remained to the growers at the war's end. 1928 and 1929 were great years, but the 1930's, with two exceptions, were disappointing, and even though 1942 was a fair year and 1943 a good one, the general derangement meant that the wines came to birth with something less than their usual ease. Fortune favored the growers immediately by giving them three great years, 1945, 1947, and 1949, with the intervening years better than average; but demand had risen also and to recoup their losses and restock their cellars, vinification methods in many vineyards began to be changed to push the wines to quick maturity. Justification for this course is of the realistic kind: it ensures the growers an early return for their efforts, and it is in vehement agreement with the views stated on page 31, which compare modern living conditions with the more serene and leisurely prevailing before the 1914-18 war.

Many years ago most of us took note of the number of wines which arrived on our shores decanted before shipping, the loss being the sediment heavy with life-sustaining substances which enables a wine to mature to its full and natural stature, and now one hears of more ominous alterations in the traditional methods of wine-making. To one who has not participated in the wine-making process, the technical terms involved in the change present less than the complete picture, but even a small understanding of them adds up to an over-all curtailment, resulting in a sophisticated softness permitting early bottling and almost immediate consumption. The laws of each country take note of the sleights-of-hand employed, but, as an eminent French wine-grower once said, the laws are splendid; it is in their enforcement that they falter.

As a consequence of this upheaval, we are instructed to drink the great wines at five years or younger, because no longer can one expect their quality to increase much beyond. Whether this advice proclaims cynical opportunism or indisputable fact, in which case no reliance can be placed on former opinion as to standards in wine, is a query best put to the aforementioned trustworthy wine-merchant, whose business it is to know not only the degrees of excellence as between vineyards, but also the changes taking place in the wines themselves as they develop. And there is always one's own taste to consult. Buy single bottles of your favorite wines, and decide what, if any, future you can discern for them.

The pre-taste by single bottle is a wise precaution in the purchase of this wine. A too young one may be a singularly unpleasant dose.

1945, 1947, 1949 were all great years, the '45's and the '47's slow to mature, the '49's recommended for early drinking. There were surprisingly good '48's and '50's. 1952 and 1953 produced great wines, the '53's early maturing, and the '52's somewhat reluctant. The 1954's were fair, the 1955's splendid wines, early maturing but not ready to drink, and the small crop of '57's are better than average, developing slowly. The 1959's seem destined to please everyone.

Aging, it must be said, at no time guaranteed properties of fineness unless they were inherent in the wine. Aging merely ensured the wine a proper chance to declare itself.

MÉDOC CLARETS

The Official Classification of 1855

It is important not to confuse lesser classifications of Bordeaux with the classification of the best growths listed below. Each commune has its own classification apart from the Médoc Classification. For example, a Château Calon-Ségur, a Third *Cru* Médoc, has printed on its label *"Premier Cru de Saint-Estèphe—Médoc."* Also districts not represented on this or any other official classification have their own gradings into *crus*. Such secondary designations must not be mistaken for the *Crus Classés* of the Médoc.

One additional warning: Wines grown in the Commune of Margaux often display that name so prominently that the actual name and class of the wine fail to be noted. The lesser wines of the commune should not be confused with the one and only Margaux.

Premiers Crus (FIRST GROWTHS)

Château Lafite-Rothschild-Pauillac
Château Latour-Pauillac

Château Margaux-Margaux
Château Haut-Brion-Graves

Deuxièmes Crus (SECOND GROWTHS)

Château Mouton-Rothschild	Pauillac
Château Rausan-Ségla	Margaux
Château Rauzan-Gassies	Margaux
Château Léoville-Las Cases	Saint Julien
Château Léoville-Poyferré	Saint Julien
Château Léoville-Barton	Saint Julien
Château Durfort-Vivens	Margaux
Château Lascombes	Margaux
Château Gruaud-Larose	Saint Julien
Château Brane-Cantenac	Cantenac
Château Pichon-Longueville	Pauillac
Château Pichon-Longueville-Comtesse de Lalande	Pauillac
Château Ducru-Beaucaillou	Saint Julien
Château Cos d'Estournel	Saint Estèphe
Château Montrose	Saint Estèphe

Troisièmes Crus (THIRD GROWTHS)

Château Kirwan	Cantenac
Château d'Issan	Cantenac
Château Lagrange	Saint Julien
Château Langoa-Barton	Saint Julien
Château Giscours	Labarde
Château Malescot-Saint-Exupéry	Margaux
Château Cantenac-Brown	Cantenac
Château Palmer	Margaux
Château Grand-La-Lagune	Ludon
Château Desmirail	Margaux
Château Calon-Ségur	Saint Estèphe
Château Ferrière	Margaux
Château Marquis-d'Alesme-Becker	Margaux
Château Boyd-Cantenac	Margaux

Quatrièmes Crus (FOURTH GROWTHS)

Château Saint-Pierre	Saint Julien
Château Branaire-Ducru	Saint Julien
Château Talbot	Saint Julien
Château Duhart-Milon	Pauillac
Château Pouget	Cantenac
Château La Tour-Carnet	Saint Laurent
Château Rochet	Saint Estèphe
Château Beychevelle	Saint Julien
Château Prieuré-Lichine	Cantenac
Château Marquis-de-Terme	Margaux

Cinquièmes Crus (FIFTH GROWTHS)

Château Pontet-Canet	Pauillac
Château Batailley	Pauillac
Château Grand-Puy-Lacoste	Pauillac
Château Grand-Puy-Ducasse	Pauillac
Château Lynch-Bages	Pauillac
Château Lynch-Moussas	Pauillac
Château Dauzac	Labarde
Château Mouton-d'Armailhacq	
	Pauillac
Château du Tertre	Arsac
Château Haut-Bages-Libéral	Pauillac
Château Pedesclaux	Pauillac
Château Belgrave	Saint Laurent
Château Camensac	Saint Laurent
Château Cos-Labory	Saint Estèphe
Château Clerc-Milon-Mondon	
	Pauillac
Château Croizet-Bages	Pauillac
Château Cantemerle	Macau

GRAVES

1953 Official Classification

Château Bouscaut	Château Haut-Brion
Château Carbonnieux	Château La Mission-Haut-
Domaine de Chevalier	Brion
Château Couhins	Château La Tour-Haut-
Château Haut-Bailly	Brion

GRAVES—*continued*

Château La Tour-Martillac
Château Malartic-
    Lagravière
Château Olivier

Château Pape Clément
Château Smith-Haut-
    Lafitte

SAINT EMILION

1955 Official Classification

First Classified Great Growths

Château Ausone
Château Cheval Blanc
Château Beauséjour-
    Lagarosse
Château Beauséjour-
    Fagouet
Château Belair
Château Canon

Château Clos Fourtet
Château Figeac
Château La Gaffelière
    Naudes
Château Magdelaine
Château Pavie
Château Trottevieille

Great Classified Growths

Château L'Angelus
Château Balestard la
    Tonnelle
Château Bellevue
Château Bergat
Château Cadet Bon
Château Cadet Piola

Château Canon la
    Gaffelière
Château Cap de Mourlin
Château Chapelle
    Madeleine
Château Chauvin
Château Corbin

SAINT EMILION—*continued*

Great Classified Growths—continued

Château Corbin Michotte
Château Coutet
Château Croque Michotte
Château Cure Bon
Château Fonplegade
Château Fonroque
Château Franc Mayne
Château Grand Barrail
  Lamarzelle Figeac
Château Grand Corbin
  Despagne
Château Grand Corbin
  Pecresse
Château Grand Mayne
Château Grand Pontet
Château Grandes Murailles
Château Guadet Saint Julien
Château Jean Faure
Château Clos des Jacobins
Château La Carte
Château La Clotte
Château La Couspaude
Château La Dominique
Château Clos La
  Madeleine
Château Larcis Ducasse
Château Lamarzelle
Château Larmande
Château Laroze

Château Lasserre
Château La Tour du Pin
  Figeac
Château La Tour Figeac
Château Le Chatelet
Château Le Couvent
Château Le Prieuré
Château Mauvezin
Château Moulin du Cadet
Château Pavie Decesse
Château Pavie Macquin
Château Pavillon Cadet
Château Petit Faurie de
  Souchard
Château Petit Faurie de
  Soutard
Château Ripeau
Château Sansonnet
Château Saint Georges
  Côte Pavie
Château Clos Saint Martin
Château Soutard
Château Tertre Daugay
Château Trimoulet
Château Trois Moulins
Château Troplong Mondot
Château Villemaurine
Château Yon Figeac

POMEROL

Château Pétrus

Château Beauregard
Château Clinet
Château Feytit-Clinet
Château Gazin
Château Guillot
Château La Conseillante
Château La Croix
Château La Croix-de-Gay
Château Lafleur
Château Lagrange
Château la Grave-Trigant-
   de-Boisset

Château La Pointe
Château Latour-Pomerol
Château L'Evangile
Château Le Gay
Château Nénin
Château Petit-Village
Château Rouget
Château Trotanoy
Clos L'Eglise
Clos L'Eglise-Clinet
Vieux Château Certan

∽ ∽

WHITE BORDEAUX

Which is the finer, white Burgundy or white Bordeaux?

In this field there can be little argument. No groups of wine differ more widely in all respects than these. Granted a fine white wine from either region, the Burgundy will be dry and the flavor complex; the Bordeaux, a Sauternes probably, will be sweet and its bouquet will be filled with sunshine and the multiple scents of the grape.

The principal white wines of Bordeaux come from three districts: Sauternes, Barsac, and Graves.

SAUTERNES

The wines of Sauternes are sweet and the finest of them hold first rank among the great natural sweet wines of the world. In this district there is a special method of wine-making designed to produce a type, and if one can believe a very plausible-sounding legend, an accident was responsible for its discovery. According to custom, the vintage was not begun until the master of the vineyard was in residence. In the time of a later Louis, XIV or XV, the master of the vineyard of Château d'Yquem was delayed at the court in Paris, and at the vineyard the workers wrung their hands and danced in agony as they watched the grapes burst and shrivel in the sun and become covered with mold. When the master arrived—memory has him pounding up on a blown horse—the vintage was made, in the hope that all would prove not to be lost. The result was the first of the great sweet wines of Bordeaux.

A somewhat similar legend concerns the making of the remarkable sweet *Trockenbeeren Auslesen*, except that in the case of these great wines of Germany, it was a Bishop who erred.

However begun, the method of allowing the grapes to become overripe on the vine has been followed in both regions, and in good years when the weather is right—that is, when the sun is hot and the rains hold off—the grapes when picked contain such a wealth of sugar that a portion only is transformed into alcohol. The rest remains to sweeten the wine. The selection of the grapes for pressing is an important matter. The picking is done over a period of weeks, only grapes of a certain degree of over-ripeness or "noble rottenness" being taken each time. The wines from the first pickings become *vins de tête*, the finest of them being labeled *Crême de tête*. The proprietor of Château d'Yquem, the Marquis de Lur-Saluces, made a *Crême de tête* in 1921 which was as fine a wine of this type as I ever tasted. It was taking on the brownish *"maderisé"* tone, and was like honey, rich and beautiful.

The wines of Sauternes, including those of Barsac, have been officially classified and Château d'Yquem stands alone in a special classification at the head of the list. While this rating is undoubtedly justified, there are other growths that follow Yquem closely and in some cases seem to step ahead. Château Suduiraut has a hint of nutty flavor along with sweetness that is distinguishing and exceedingly pleasant; Château Rieussec, more complex than Yquem, is very near in merit; Château Lafaurie-Peyraguey is a charming wine, its bouquet perhaps not quite up to that of Yquem; and Clos Haut-Peyraguey has maintained a quality both constant and fine.

A thing which it is well to understand about Sauternes is this: that because of its sweetness a fine Sauternes of a good year is too syrupy to be drunk except with dessert, and preferably a dessert in which the sugar ingredient is kept low. Therefore those who wish to drink Sauternes with a meal should buy an ordinary Sauternes or Haut Sauternes of no vintage year. Both are easy to find in very acceptable quality, as I learned while tasting hundreds of wines in preparation for the making of the Hotel St. Regis winelist. They are quite similar but the Haut-Sauternes are bigger and have a fuller flavor than the Sauternes.

Perhaps the ultimate in the serving of the great sweet wines is practiced at Château d'Yquem, where, to honor favored guests, the Marquis has the wine frozen for three days and serves only the small portion left in liquid form, a kind of heavenly essence.

BARSAC

The characteristic taste of Barsacs is often described as "rusty." These wines are in general less sweet than the Sauternes and they have a good deal of flavor. The best of them are the Châteaux Climens and Coutet, two wines especially beautiful in good years, big and fruity, approaching the great Sauternes in excellence. All are listed and sold as Sauternes. Lesser Barsacs, labeled simply Barsac or Barsac Supérieur, make pleasant luncheon wines if you can find good ones. As with the district Médocs, the soundest carry a vintage year and the name of a dependable shipper.

WHITE GRAVES

Graves derives its name from the gravel soil in which it grows. This gravel tends to give the wine, when it is at its best, a clean, flinty taste faintly suggesting that of certain Rhine wines, but less pronounced. Too often, however, the wine seems to have not a clean but an acid taste, or perhaps one could call it an astringent quality. Blending can often smooth down the rough edges, and in this particular instance, I have come to prefer a blend. Graves are the driest white wines of Bordeaux, and the driest of them all is Château Carbonnieux, one of the notable wines of the district. Years ago a topside Turk, a former ambassador to France, used to have shipped to him in Turkey large quantities of Château Carbonnieux. Being a Moslem, the drinking of wine was forbidden him, but the "out" in this case was that, as shown by its name, the stuff was not wine but a sort of carbonated beverage.

Other good wines are Château Laville-Haut-Brion, Domaine de Chevalier, Château Olivier, and Château Bouscaut.

Graves and Barsacs are considerably less expensive than Sauternes.

VINTAGE YEARS IN WHITE BORDEAUX

Generally speaking, white wines may be drunk much younger than reds. This is not true of the foremost among the Sauternes, which remain for several years in cask before bottling and require some age to mellow their almost too great sweetness. Good wines of this type made in the notable years 1953 and 1955 may still be found. The very great 1945's and 1947's and the very good 1949's and 1952's are little now but facts to record. The '56's and '57's were fair only and should be bought with care. Many of the lighter wines are bottled within the year of vintage and can be delicious. The good 1958's and the great 1959's may be bought with confidence.

PRINCIPAL WHITE BORDEAUX SAUTERNES AND BARSAC

Grand Premier Cru (GRAND FIRST GROWTH)

Château d'Yquem

Premiers Crus (FIRST GROWTHS)

Château Rayne-Vigneau
Château La Tour Blanche
Château Suduiraut
Château Climens
Château Coutet

Clos Haut-Peyraguey
Château Lafaurie-Peyraguey
Château Guiraud
Château Rieussec
Château Rabaud-Promis

Château Sigalas-Rabaud

~~~~~~

Deuxièmes Crus (SECOND GROWTHS)

Château Mirat   Château Broustet
Château Doisy-Daëne   Château Nairac
Château Doisy-Dubroca   Château Caillou
Château Doisy-Védrines   Château Suau
Château D'Arche   Château Malle
Château Filhot   Château Romer

Château Lamothe

GRAVES

Château Bouscaut   Château Laville-Haut-Brion
Château Carbonnieux   Château La Tour-Martillac
Domaine de Chevalier   Château Olivier

∽ ∽

BURGUNDY WINES

The prestige of Burgundy wines goes back to Roman days, and the great Burgundies, both red and white, have been more widely praised by the good and great, throughout the ages, than any other wines. As mentioned earlier, a meal in which a fine red Burgundy is served with other wines must climax with the red Burgundy, which has a flavor so rich, round, and beautifully assertive as to kill the flavors of more delicate wines if they are served after it. The best white Burgundies are rated by many good judges the greatest dry white wines in existence, their only possible competitors being the Ausleses and Cabinet Rhines of great years.

The main Burgundy region has two principal divisions. At its northern extremity is the low range of hills, something more than thirty miles in length, that drop down the map in a southwesterly direction from the ancient wine towns of Nuits and Beaune, to the village of Chagny. These are the hills of the famous Côte d'Or, or Slope of Gold, in the chalky soil of which grows, better than anywhere else in the world, the Pinot grape, in both its black and its white varieties.

The Côte d'Or is divided into three sections. At the north is the Côte de Dijon. The center section is the Côte de Nuits, and the southern end the Côte de Beaune. The second division of Burgundy is another low range of hills south of the Côte d'Or, the Côtes of Chalon, Mâcon, and Beaujolais following one after the other to just north of Lyon where the Saône flows into the Rhône. Each of these latter districts produces very pleasant and often distinguished wines, but the Côte d'Or is the big show. A third district, the small vineyard area of Chablis, some eighty miles northwest of the Côte d'Or, produces a highly distinctive dry white wine that at its best adds substantially to Burgundy's glory.

The wine-growing districts of Bordeaux and Burgundy differ in an important fundamental: whereas the Bordeaux vineyards are large and belong almost always to individuals or families who see to the cultivation of their grapes and the making of their wine, the vineyards of the Côte d'Or are divided among some 1,800 wine-growers, and of these, 1,400 have properties averaging less than two and a half acres.

RED BURGUNDY

RED WINES OF THE CÔTE D'OR

The Côte de Dijon at one time produced fine wines, but at the present time none of its wines is widely known with the exception of Clos de la Perrière, sometimes mentioned among the great red Burgundies. I don't remember ever having tasted it or seen it in this country.

The Côte de Nuits

Precisely as the Côte d'Or is the jewel of Burgundy, so the Côte de Nuits is the inner jewel of the Côte d'Or. Its hillsides are given over to the cultivation of the black Pinot grape from which the noblest red Burgundies are without exception made. The Pinot is a cranky grape; it grows best in sheltered, sunny places midway up the slope, and the quality of the wine it yields sometimes varies greatly within a single small vineyard, to say nothing of the larger ones. Lesser red Burgundies, some of them very good, are made from the Gamay, which produces flavors less full and fruity than the Pinot and a bouquet lacking in sumptuousness. It was surely the

juice of the Pinot that inspired Dumas to declare that
the wines of the Côte d'Or should be drunk kneel-
ing and bareheaded.

With but few exceptions, the greatest red Burgundies are grown in the Côte de Nuits. The famous
vineyards follow one another down the length of the
slope: Chambertin, Clos de Bèze, Clos de Tart,
Bonnes-Mares, Musigny, Clos de Vougeot, Grands
Échézeaux, Richebourg, Romanée Conti, La Tâche,
Romanée St. Vivant, St. Georges, and others.

Romanée Conti, grown on a vineyard of only four
and a half acres, was by common consent rated the
greatest of all red Burgundies, and that to many
wine-lovers meant the greatest of all wines. It is a
wine always associated with high station and high
functions. The Prince de Conti is said to have once
owned the vineyard, and Madame de Maintenon
tried without success to buy it. In the old days much
of the understandably limited quantity of this great
wine went into royal and ducal cellars, and most of
the rest of us can count the occasions when we've
been served it. In 1928 only two or three restaurants
in Paris listed Romanée Conti, and my recollection
is that the price was somewhere in the neighborhood
of thirty dollars a bottle. In 1935 I gave a dinner in
Hollywood to star just one bottle—a magnificent
1915. A roast peacock in all its glory shared honors,
but the wine was as great as one can taste, and nothing could compete. Except for the few times in wine-
tastings when bottles have been corked or otherwise

not kept well, it never failed to be what it was, the noblest Roman of them all, possessed of the almost spicy quality that was the hallmark of the wine.

The pre-phylloxera vines at Romanée Conti were torn out after the 1945 vintage, the plot planted to ungrafted vines. The first of the new wines was tasted in cask in 1952, and while the hope is that the wines will regain their former authority as the vines develop strength, present opinion rates them as light, their future promise still in question.

Chambertin, second in popular favor, may generally be given top marks for quality, those designated *Tout Court* being especially fine. It is a mascule wine, dignified, not so soft, and possibly not so fruity, as the wines of Vosne-Romanée. Among the great ones Richebourg, an impressive wine, must not be overlooked. Romanée St. Vivant and La Tâche can be full and lovely; and Grands Échézeaux proclaims a kinship with its aristocratic neighbors. The vineyard of Clos de Vougeot is claimed by some to be the finest in Burgundy and to produce the finest wines. Musigny and Bonnes-Mares, rather lighter than the "big" Burgundies, are delightful wines of rare race and breed. Incidentally, several of the vineyards have small plantings of pre-phylloxera vines, how preserved in the general debacle no one knows. It is generally conceded that the wines made of the old vines are of finer quality than those made from the new. The distinguishing mark for the rare Richebourg *vieux cépages* is *Vigne Originelle Française non Reconstituée,* printed just below the name, and the Chambertin old vines are owned by the Latours and the truly magnificent wine is designated *Cuvée Héritiers Latour.*

A part of the fame of Chambertin is due undoubtedly to the constant mention of the wine in Napoleonic memoirs. None but a very great wine could have stood the hardship and adversity Napoleon demanded of it. Wherever he went he carried his Chambertin and his Burgundy wine-merchant to look after it. Writes Bourienne, his private secretary on the Egyptian campaign:

> In this campaign we had an opportunity to ascertain that good Burgundy, well racked off and in sealed casks, does not lose its quality on a sea voyage. Several boxes of this Burgundy twice crossed the desert on camel-back and some which we brought with us on our return to Fréjus was as good as when we started.

On the Russian campaign, and even through most of the retreat from Moscow, Napoleon had his Burgundy. General de Coulaincourt's diary notes: ". . . Only the Emperor had been well served throughout the retreat: that is to say, he always had white bread, linen, his Chambertin. . . ."

One of the most interesting wines I ever tasted was a Chambertin 1906 drunk in 1942. This was a bottle of the famous "Cachet de Liége" wines that had been concealed in a subcellar of a brewery in Liége, Belgium, during the 1914-18 war and subsequently shipped to London. Its color was superb and its bouquet made me think of what perfume would be like if there were a perfume made of wine. In taste it was velvet smooth, but it was old, old velvet, just a little faded but all the more precious for that. Actually its thirty-six years made it too old for a Burgundy except as a curio, but it was a "beautiful widow" par excellence.

Clos de Bèze is usually bottled as Chambertin, the label sometimes carrying the name "Chambertin Clos de Bèze." The vineyards adjoin and the wines are almost identical.

In fine years, and even in years less than fine, splendid wines are made in the secondary vineyards of the Côte de Nuits, listed under First Group wines of the various communes. They are less expensive than the wines of the Supreme First Group, and when well bought are extremely pleasant. I refer to such wines as Morey, Clos de la Roche and Clos de Lambrays, Gevrey-Chambertin, Clos St. Jacques, Chambolle-Musigny, Les Amoureuses.

The Côte de Beaune

The Côte de Beaune section of the Côte d'Or can proudly point to two vineyards once owned by Charlemagne. Both are in the parish of Aloxe-Corton: One, Clos du Roi, produces a nice red wine, and the other, Charlemagne, one of the really noteworthy white wines of the world.

The chief glory of the Côte de Beaune is its white wines, but the region grows some fine reds. In broad comparison with the wines of the Côte de Nuits, the reds of the Côte de Beaune may be said to be lighter in body but to have greater delicacy, to mature earlier, and, except in rare years, to lack at their peak something of the grand dimensions of the reds grown just to the north. Once the accepted age for drinking these wines was from six to nine years, with an occasional bottle continuing to develop to a nice age: an Aloxe-Corton, Les Vercots 1928, tasted in January 1947, was delicately finished and promised to continue so for years to come; and a Corton, Clos du Roi 1923, drunk in 1945, was a fine wine in excellent condition. Recent vintages in the Côte de Beaune have produced wines destined for early drinking.

The more notable red wines of this district are grown in Aloxe-Corton, Volnay, Chassagne-Montrachet and Meursault; also Pernand-Vergelesses, Savigny, Beaune, Pommard, Monthélie, and Santenay. The vineyards listed under the First Group must not be disregarded. Many make great wines.

The twenty-eight vineyards owned by the Hospices de Beaune are all in the Côte de Beaune. Six produce white wines, the remaining, red wines. Prices at the annual auction of Hospices de Beaune wines are considered generally to reflect wine-trade opinion of the previous year's Burgundy vintage. Beaune is Burgundy's wine capital, and the ancient buildings of the Hospices de Beaune are its great point of interest. They consist of a stately poorhouse and hospital built in 1443 by Nicolas Rolin, Chancellor of the Duchy of Burgundy in the time of Philip the Good. The wealth of the Hospices is in vineyards, and the auction of casks of wine, held annually on the second Sunday in November, is Burgundy's great wine event. A picturesque feature of the auction, which is usually attended by dealers from many lands, is bidding by candle. When a lot is put up, a wax taper is lighted; bidding continues while the taper burns, and stops when it goes out. The wines are not bottled at the Hospices. Each purchaser, however, is given corks and labels for the bottling, the number corresponding exactly to the quantity of wine that has been sold him. Since the wines from the twenty-eight vineyards differ in kind and excellence, they should be bought only under expert guidance.

VINTAGE YEARS IN RED BURGUNDY

Burgundies require less bottle age than Clarets, but, as with Clarets, they should not be drunk too young despite the present tendency to persuade both the wine and the drinkers of them into early consumption. The wines of the lesser years may be enjoyed young, and the same is true of the *vins de com-*

mune. Big wines are another matter. The wines of 1945 and 1947 were superb, with the '49's only a shade less so. However, little if any is left. Without ample stocks of older years to draw on, we have been getting through the wines of the great post-war years too fast.

In Burgundy, as in Bordeaux, 1952 and 1953 were great years. The 1953's were not only charming but precocious, and matured rapidly. They may be shorter-lived than the '52's, which are taking more time about it. Fair wines were made in 1950 and in 1954. 1955 produced some excellent wines, but the yield was not uniform; 1956, with its black frosts in February and May, was almost a complete disaster. The wines were so poor that for the first time in years the November auction at the Hospices de Beaune was not held. Wines of quality which will be slow in maturing were made in 1957; the 1958's were below average, and again the 1959's draw out all superlatives.

In any vintage discussion the wines of the earlier great years should have mention at least: 1926, 1928 and 1929, 1934, 1937, and 1943. Only small amounts of each remain, in private cellars or occasionally offered for sale as great prizes by enterprising wine merchants. The last of our own '26's and '28's were opened recently, and despite their considerable age they were soft, still fragrant, and beautiful. It is interesting to note the attitude of guests who are served wines of this perfection: all grow still. There are no words to use in description, and seldom is one sought. Tasting is solitary business, and never is that fact so well demonstrated as on such occasions.

RED BURGUNDIES OF THE CÔTE D'OR

CÔTE DE DIJON

Tête de Cuvée
(SUPREME FIRST GROWTH)

Clos de la Perrière

CÔTE DE NUITS

Tête de Cuvée
(SUPREME FIRST GROWTH)

Chambertin	Romanée Conti
Clos de Bèze	Romanée St. Vivant
Clos de Tart	Romanée, La
Musigny	Richebourg
Bonnes-Mares	La Tâche
Clos de Vougeot	St. Georges
Grands Échézeaux	Les Cailles

First Growth

Commune of Gevrey- *Chambertin*	
Clos St. Jacques	Les Ruchottes
Les Latricières	Aux Charmes
	La Chapelle

CÔTE DE NUITS—*continued*

First Growth—continued

Commune of Morey
　Les Millandes
　Clos de la Roche
　Les Bouchots
　Les Lambrays
　Clos St. Denis
Commune of Chambolle-
　　Musigny
　Les Amoureuses
　Les Petits Musigny
　Les Charmes
Commune of Vougeot
　Les Petits Vougeots
Commune of Flagey-
　　Échézeaux
　Les Champs
　Les Échézeaux du
　　Dessus
　En Orveaux
　Les Poulaillières

Commune of Vosne-
　　Romanée
　Les Gaudichots
　Les Beaumonts
　Les Suchots
　Grande Rue
　Les Malconsorts
Commune of Nuits-Saint
　　Georges
　Les Poirets
　Les Pruliers
　La Perrière
　Aux Murgers
　Les Vaucrains
　Aux Boudots
Commune of Prémeaux
　Les Corvées
　Les Forêts
　Les Didiers

CÔTE DE BEAUNE

Tête de Cuvée
(SUPREME FIRST GROWTH)

Corton
Corton Clos du Roi
Les Grèves

Les Fèves
Pommard-Rugiens
Volnay en Caillerets

Meursault Les Santenots

CÔTE DE BEAUNE—*continued*

First Growth

Commune of Aloxe-Corton
En Charlemagne
Les Renardes
Les Bressandes
Les Pougets
Les Perrières
Les Grèves
La Vigne au Saint

Commune of Pernand-
Vergelesses
Ile des Vergelesses
Les Basses Vergelesses
Les Fichots

Commune of Savigny
Aux Gravains
Les Jarrons
Les Marconnets

Commune of Beaune
Clos des Mouches
Les Aigrots
Les Cent Vignes
Les Bressandes
Les Marconnets
Les Cras
Les Vigne Franches
Les Perrières
Les Toussaints
Les Champs Pimonts
Clos de la Mousse

Commune of Pommard
Les Arvelets
Les Épenots
Les Pézerolles
Les Fremiers
Les Jarollières
Les Croix Noires
Les Bertins
Les Poutures
Les Sausilles

Commune of Volnay
Les Champans
Les Mitans
Clos de Frémiet
Les Angles
La Chapelle
Clos des Ducs
En Chevret

Commune of Monthélie
Les Cras Rougeot
Les Champs Fulliot

Commune of Meursault
Blagny
Les Cras
Les Pelures

Commune of Puligny-
Montrachet
Le Cailleret

CÔTE DE BEAUNE—*continued*

First Growth—continued

Commune of Chassagne-	Les Morgeots
Montrachet	Les Chaumées
Clos St. Jean	*Commune of Santenay*
La Boudriotte	Les Gravières

WHITE BURGUNDY

WHITE WINES OF THE COTE D'OR

Just as the very great red Burgundies come from the Côte de Nuits, the very great whites come principally from the adjoining Côte de Beaune. There are, however, three superb white wines made in famous vineyards of the red wine regions, bearing the names usually associated with great red wines. Of these, Clos Blanc de Vougeot and La Romanée Blanche, produced in very small quantity, are rarely met with. Musigny Blanc is sometimes to be found. All are worth searching for.

The Côte de Beaune

The white wines of the Côte de Beaune are, at their best, beyond all praise. They were the favorite wines of men as various as Louis XV, Du Guesclin, François Villon, and Buffon, and they rate high with all discriminating wine-lovers. Incomparably the greatest is Montrachet—"divine Montrachet," as it was long ago called and has been called ever since.

In white wines like Montrachet and reds like Chambertin, the collaboration of God and man in works of art is beautifully apparent. Even Shand becomes lyric when he writes of Montrachet:

> What can be said of this peerless wine . . . save that its name is fair as its fame? The wonderful flavor of Château d'Yquem is soon drowned in the syrupy flood of unfermented grape-sugar, while Montrachet is rich and luscious as it is vast and grand from the first sip to the last reflex of the after-taste, but without a trace of cloying sweetness. . . .

This is precisely the fact, and the Marquis de la Guiche, the Baron Thénard, and other proprietors of the vineyard, have jealously guarded its honor. A thing to remember about Montrachet is that it lies in two communes, Chassagne and Puligny. The best Montrachet comes from Puligny.

Montrachet overshadows certain other fine wines produced near by. The vineyards of Chevalier-Montrachet and Bâtard-Montrachet grow splendid wines, only a step behind Montrachet in good years. The same is true of Les Combettes. The wines of Meursault, when well selected, can be very pleasant, and the delightful Corton-Charlemagne has already been mentioned. And included in this top listing must be a wine from the southern district of Mâconnais, able to sing with the best of them, Pouilly-Fuissé. In the summer of 1946 I opened a bottle of Pouilly-Fuissé 1928 which had risen from a very good but rather hard white Burgundy to a perfection of balance, fragrance, might, and deep amber color that made it almost the twin and certainly the equal of many Montrachets. It was a lesson in what time could do to a fine wine.

The experience of many tastings of Meursault has shown that to be really good a Meursault must have a vineyard name coupled with it—Meursault-Charmes, -Perrières, -Goutte d'Or, -Genevrières. A wine labeled simply Meursault can be anything—out of the vineyards of Meursault, it's true, but seldom reliable.

For serving, cool these great white wines but do not ice them. Icing robs them of fragrance and charm. A proper cellar temperature, about 55°, or slightly cooler, is right for them.

VINTAGE YEARS
IN WHITE BURGUNDIES

One of the great wine-growers of Burgundy has declared his white wines to be at their best at four years. If one agrees with this opinion, the fine wines of 1945 and 1949 and the great wines of 1947 may be disregarded along with the fair ones of 1946 and 1948, which tended to be overlooked because of their luckless position. The '50's were surprisingly good; the '53's early maturing, the '52's slightly the best of the great twins, 1952 and 1953; and the '54's were passable. 1955 produced excellent wines on the forward side; 1956 little of note; and although quantity was disappointingly small in 1957, quality was very pleasant. 1958 was a fair year only, and 1959 may be the best year of the century.

The listing that follows does not pretend to include more than those of high merit.

CHOICE WHITE WINES OF THE CÔTE DE BEAUNE

Grand Premier Cru (GRAND FIRST GROWTH)

Montrachet, *Grand Vin*

Premiers Crus (FIRST GROWTHS)

Chevalier-Montrachet	Meursault-Charmes
Bâtard-Montrachet	Meursault-Goutte d'Or
Les Combettes	Blagny Blanc
Meursault-Perrières	Corton Blanc
Meursault-Genevrières	Clos Blanc de Vougeot

Corton-Charlemagne

CHABLIS

Before continuing our way to the southward for a look at the three adjoining sections outranked by the Côte d'Or, we shall leave the main Burgundy wine region and travel some eighty miles to the northwest, to the district of Chablis, famous for its dry white Burgundies. The wine of Chablis was known in the ninth century; for more than a hundred years it has been the wine par excellence to drink with oysters—if you like wine with oysters. Undoubtedly if one must have wine with oysters a Chablis is more suitable than the Sauternes that used to be considered proper at New York dinners.

Authentic Chablis has a special fragrance and a characteristic "gunflint" flavor. Unlike other white wines, Chablis does not become darker with age, but retains a bright yellow color slightly tinged with green. While not a sturdy wine, it can live pleasantly to quite an age. A Chablis Grenouille 1919 uncorked in 1944 was a big wine for a Chablis, 1919 having been a great year in this wine. It was anything but tired, and unquestionably would have retained its character and quality for ten or fifteen years. This, however, was another of the exceptions one must register constantly when writing of wines. Generally a Chablis loses in age some of the delicacy and lightness it has when young.

Chablis is always scarce and always high-priced— this because the true Chablis area, on the hillsides of the right bank of the Serein, is not more than three-quarters of a mile long. The best grades carry a vineyard name, such as Chablis-Vaudésir, -Grenouille, -Blanchot, -Valmur; or a proprietary name such as Moutonne, which may be very good. Wines from outside the inner Chablis area formerly known as *Chablis Village* or *Chablis Supèrieure*, and later as plain *Chablis,* are now known as *Petit-Chablis.* They were not recommended under their former designations and are not recommended now except on trusted advice. They are made from the white Pinot grape but seldom reveal the charming qualities that make the fine Chablis so much admired.

A fact not commonly known is that the wine of Chablis, like Moselles, Vouvrays, and Seyssel from Savoy, sometimes turns sleepily sparkling in the spring, as if it remembered the sap stirring in the vine. The French speak of a wine thus gently prickling as being *pétillant*, in contradistinction to *mousseaux*, which means a wine that is made to sparkle by artificial process, such as that employed in the manufacture of Champagne and the detestable Sparkling Burgundy.

It has been said that no one but a Frenchman and a fine judge of wine knows how to buy good Chablis, and it is fair to assume that the same rule applies to the buying of Côte d'Or wines. The buyer goes to the grower, samples wines from different barrels in his cellar, selects the wine he likes best, haggles over the price, and finally comes to terms. He does not then go away and send a truck to get the barrel he has bought, but carts it away at once, knowing well that if he fails to do so, the grower is likely to tap the barrel, draw off half the contents, and fill the barrel with inferior wine.

The vintage years in Chablis are similar to those of the Burgundy district with the important difference that because of its more northerly position there are fewer fine years. Bad frosts occur with too great frequency, and sometimes mean near disaster. While

Chablis in age can be a beautiful wine, it is delicious when drunk young.

THE IMPORTANT
CHABLIS DESIGNATIONS

The principal growths of Chablis are as follows:

(SUPREME FIRST GROWTH)

Blanchot
Les Clos
Valmur
Grenouille
Vaudésir

(FIRST GROWTH)

Mont de Milieu
Chapelot
Montée de Tonnerre
Pointes des Preuses
Bougros
Fourchaume
Vaulorent

(SECOND GROWTH)

Les Forêts
Montmain
Beugnon
Vaillon
Melinots
Roncières
Les Lys
Séchet
Epinotte
Vaucoupin
Côte de Lechet
Beauroy
Troëmes
Côte de Fontenay

LESSER BURGUNDIES,
RED AND WHITE

Chalonnais—Mâconnais—Beaujolais

The glamour of the Côte d'Or tends sometimes, in the eyes of foreigners, to place the Chalonnais, Mâconnais, and Beaujolais districts, by contrast, in the shade, but he who overlooks them must overlook as well some very good and useful wines, and certain clean-cut growers who have large vineyards and who take pride in their product and do their own bottling. The wines of these South Burgundian regions are generally reasonable in price.

THE CHALONNAIS produces a large amount of both red and white wines, the best known being the red Mercurey. It is made principally of the Pinot grape, and while light, is fragrant and can be very good. Selection here is important, as the yield is uneven in quality.

THE MÂCONNAIS is famed for the fresh and agreeable white wine called Pouilly or Pouilly-Fuissé, already mentioned under White Burgundy. Pouilly, pale gold in color, is a clean dry wine, strong when young, developing with age into a wine of superb richness. It is a long-lived wine, and at its best is a treasure. It is made of white Pinot grapes in the twin parishes of Pouilly and Fuissé. Wine is produced in the neighboring parishes of Solutré, Loché, and Chaintré, but most of it is sold as Pouilly-Fuissé.

Pouilly-Fuissé must not be confused with Pouilly-Fumé, a quite dissimilar wine from the Loire.

BEAUJOLAIS. The grape of this district is the lesser-known grape from which red Burgundy wine is made, the Gamay. This grape is a prolific bearer and will thrive almost anywhere. Many harsh things have been said of the Gamay grape. Certainly the Pinot overshadows it; certainly its juice is not worthy to be blended with that of the Pinot; certainly some of its wines are harsh and sour; but the fact should not be overlooked that under favorable circumstances it yields some very pleasant wines that generally sell at prices much lower than those brought by wines made from the Pinot. Moulin-à-Vent, a red wine generally classed as a Beaujolais although technically a Mâconnais, is made of the Gamay grape, and it is, and should be, rated *Grands Crus*. It shows how good a wine the Gamay can make. Moulin-à-Vent can stand more age than most Beaujolais.

Other well-known growths of Beaujolais are those of Fleurie (Clos de la Riolette, called "the Clos de Vougeot of Beaujolais"), Juliénas, Villié-Morgon, and Romanèche-Thorins.

Generally it may be said that good Beaujolais is a "nice" wine, fresh, light-colored, clean-flavored, lacking the richness and profundity of Côte d'Or Burgundies but very acceptable for all of that. They are especially suitable for luncheon or with a light supper. These wines do not improve with age and should be drunk very young, two years being a good age for Beaujolais. Some are drunk so young that their brief lives are spent entirely in the cask.

A number of *Vins Rosé* are made in the Beaujolais. I have never been an ardent admirer of the *rosé* wines and consequently am a bad reporter. The only one of this district I have come across was a Grand Beaujolais Rosé. It was a miserable wine, tasting like a mixture of red and white, both poor.

Fine years are rather more certain here than in Burgundy. Especially worthy of mention are the '55's and the '57's, the yield in the latter year regrettably small. The '59's will be late in maturing, as the tannin content in the must ran high.

THE PROBLEM OF BUYING BURGUNDIES

The history of the Burgundian wine lands has been long and difficult. In early Roman times the barbarians of the north used to storm out of their forests and across the Rhine to slay and plunder. They have kept coming ever since, with occasional *divertissements* by Saracens, Norsemen, and other undesirable visitors. During the French Revolution France discovered barbarians of her own. An enemy could hardly have done a more thorough job of wrecking a major French industry than did the French themselves when, in the name of liberty and justice, they expropriated the great Burgundian vineyards, most of which had belonged to the church or to important families, and allowed them to be sold off in little scraps.

The largest vineyard of the Côte d'Or, the Clos de Vougeot, with 126 acres, is the only Côte d'Or vineyard comparable in size with any one of dozens of important vineyards of the Bordeaux region. It was the pride of the monks of the Cistercian order, who cultivated it with such diligence that the fame of the wine stretched across centuries. After the confiscation

Clos de Vougeot was bought by a speculator, who cut it up and sold it in parcels, with the result that the vineyard is now owned by some forty to fifty *négociants,* or small proprietors, each entitled to call his wine by that great name. The combined vineyards of Chambertin and Clos de Bèze, 68 acres, belong to about twenty-five; the 15½ acres of Montrachet belonged, when last I investigated, to twelve. Fortunately for the reputation of Burgundy, certain of the vineyards—the smaller ones—are owned by one or, at the most, two proprietors, who make and bottle their own wines, and the wines have always been reliable. Furthermore, the entire vineyards of Romanée Conti, 4½ acres, and La Tâche, 3½ acres, along with portions of Richebourg and Grands Échézeaux were incorporated some years ago into the Domaine de la Romanée-Conti, and the owners, Messieurs de Villaine and Chambon, have upheld all traditions. It can be done and done magnificently.

Such enterprise is, however, the exception in Burgundy. Of the 1,800 proprietors in the Côte d'Or, few own as much as one acre of fine vineyard, and it is common practice for an individual to cultivate his vines and make his wine by methods differing from those of his neighbors in the same vineyard. Naturally many of the owners of small holdings do not wish to make mature wine, and the large operators who receive the grapes or the few barrels of must, being compelled in any case to blend in order to produce a marketable quantity of wine of a given standard, have sometimes been temped to bring in "foreign" wine to increase that quantity. This practice has been the root of all the trouble and is the reason why the buying of good Burgundy has presented problems. While a number of the firms have been known for well over a hundred years, and, with many of the newer houses, have reputations of honesty and probity, others have not been so high-minded, and the record of convictions for fraud in the Burgundy wine trade is not a pleasant thing to contemplate.

The convictions were secured largely through violations of a law passed in 1919 which sought to connect the true origin of a wine with the name or *appellation* carried on the label. From the point of view of regulating the trade, the legislation had little success—it served only as a rope for the hanging of culprits when they could be caught. Falsification persisted, even some of the greatest of the wines occasionally showing the deep garnet tone that means Algerian or other southern wine, and artful dodges were common. A friend once sent me a label that seems about the limit in consumer deception. The name of the wine combines two great Burgundians that have no connection of any kind—Romanée-Chambertin. Underneath is printed: *"Provenance Garantie, Mis en bouteilles en France."*

Further legislation came, another law protecting appellations of origin, *Appellation Contrôlée,* and this mark on a label is of the utmost importance to the consumer of today. To deserve the mark, a wine must be made from one or more specifically named grape varieties grown in a delimited area, varieties yielding not more than a fixed amount of wine per hectare; must have not less than 10.5% of alcoholic strength by volume; and must be made by recognized methods of wine-making. Wines conforming to the new regulations are so stamped, and since the decree covers all groupings, the stamp may be looked for not only on the great wines, but on those of the humbler classes.

In the past it has not been possible to recommend many of the district wines of Burgundy, those labeled with the commune name only, such as Nuits-St. George, Volnay, Aloxe-Corton, Gevrey-Chambertin, Pommard, and Beaune. Wine, however poor, grown in any given commune had the right to be labeled with the commune name. If such a wine was not guaranteed by a reputable grower or merchant, it was more often than not an unpleasant mixture of ordinary wines, indifferent or bad. Under the new decree, however, these wines are protected—or perhaps it is more to the point to say their consumer is protected. To be passed as authentic, they must be grown in recognized vineyards and comply in other respects with the provisions of the law.

Protection thins out in the region of wines called "Burgundy," "Côte d'Or Burgundy," "Côte de Nuits," etc. They should be bought only on expert advice.

One is likely to forget in discussing the new law

that it applies to the wines of the whole of France; also that fraud in wine districts is not confined to Burgundy. The French maintain that a great effort is being made to enforce the new regulations, both at home and with regard to exports, and while the government stamp cannot guarantee fine quality, it does hold proof of the integrity of the grower or shipper.

And in Burgundy there are other safeguards: the labels of trustworthy wines should show (1) the name of a vineyard alone if it is a great wine of the Supreme First Group—for example, *Chambertin;* and if it is of the First Group, the name of the commune and of the vineyard within the commune where the wine was grown—*Gevrey-Chambertin, Clos-St. Jacques;* (2) the year of vintage; (3) the name and address of the grower or shipper who bottled the wine. In addition, a label will sometimes carry proof of estate-bottling, such designations as *Tirage du Château, Mis en bouteilles a la propriété, Mis en bouteille au Domaine,* and *Mis en bouteilles dans mes caves.*

One complication still remains: that of the confusion in names. Many of the communes had hyphenated to their own the names of their most famous vineyards. Thus Gevrey, where Chambertin is grown, became Gevrey-Chambertin; Vosne became Vosne-Romanée; Chambolle became Chambolle-Musigny; Aloxe, Aloxe-Corton; and on through a good part of the list. Vast floods of wine go out under these twin names, to the great confusion and detriment of the innocent soul who thirsts for a good bottle and doesn't understand the racket. If you want a Chambertin, see that you get it. A Gevrey-Chambertin is not the same thing. A Chambertin is a great wine grown in the vineyard of the same name, and it will be expensive; a Gevrey-Chambertin is a district wine, which, as explained above, is one grown in a specifically recognized vineyard—or vineyards—in the commune of Gevrey, but it is not of sufficient quality to be sent out under the name of the vineyard. It should not be expensive.

It is in the buying of Burgundies that reliance must be placed on the wine-wise dealer mentioned in Chapter Two. To buy Burgundies judiciously for the American or another market requires a high degree of special knowledge, not the least important part of which is knowledge of the shipper's integrity and skill. And some understanding on the part of the buyer is always of help—to the buyer, that is. Get the names straight and don't be misled by a great name that is tangled up with another name. Learn to read labels with perception and, unless you are sure of your ground, buy no wine lacking the stamp *Appellation Contrôlée* on the label. And if you see a wine labeled "Sparkling Chambertin," get out from under.

And don't be frightened away by the complications. The plain truth is that the amount of great red Burgundy produced, or even the amount of very good red Burgundy, is only a fraction of the quantity that could be sold at good prices if it were available.

The demand is ten or twenty times greater than the supply. There are passable substitutes for Burgundy, some more than passable, but tasting a true *Grand vin* of the Côte d'Or, a great example of the ten or twelve great ones, is an experience worth having, and hunting good wines of Burgundy a pursuit immensely rewarding.

∽ ∽

RHÔNE WINES

RED RHÔNE WINES

The southern wine district of Burgundy reaches almost down to the city of Lyon, and the Rhône wine district begins just below Lyon, so that the two very nearly join.

M. Paul de Cassagnac in his excellent book, *French Wines,* deals with Rhône and other less numerous and less famous wines of France under the heading "Maids of Honor." He writes: "A Maid of Honor is not less beautiful than a Sovereign . . . but their destinies are unequal. . . . The districts which produce the Maids of Honor comprise a relatively small area. The production is inconsiderable. . . . But understand clearly, some *Maids of Honor exist which are equal to the greatest growth of our great districts.*"

All true. I first became enamored of Rhône wine

over a bottle recommended by a sommelier of a good little restaurant in Paris. That was in 1900 and the wine was a Châteauneuf-du-Pape 1887. On succeeding trips abroad I learned more of the wines from the banks of the River Rhône in their three principal varieties. These are Côte-Rôtie, produced on the rocky slopes of the right bank, just below the city of Lyon; Hermitage, further down stream on the left bank, a little way above Valence; and Châteauneuf-du-Pape, also on the left bank, a little way above Avignon, where the Popes resided from 1309 to 1376.

Rhônes are important wines, peculiarly friendly and accommodating. The Rhône Valley, being in the south, has fewer bad years than Bordeaux or Burgundy; because of this its wines are less expensive and one feels justified in using them more freely. A good red Rhône will stand up handsomely to venison, a game bird, a rabbit, or any other dish with which Burgundy or a very "big" Claret is usually associated. But whereas Burgundy is King and Claret is Queen, and Champagne is a gay old multimillionaire, the Maid of Honor from the Rhône Valley is not above sitting with you on a grassy bank and adding magic to a lunch of bread and cheese.

Both red and white wines are produced in the Valley, the reds in considerably larger quantity. Which is the best of the three great names? Choice depends on the year, the weather, and the vinification. Many tastings have caused me to rate Côte-Rôtie first, but I've been known to change my mind and prefer a

Châteauneuf when it was great and all of a piece.

Rhônes are likely when young to be harsh and even bitter, and must have age to be known at their best. It can almost be said that no wine improves so much in bottle, and despite the new preoccupation with early drinking, a big Rhône must be given time to lose its harshness. A 1926 Côte-Rôtie served to guests in the spring of 1960 had aged magnificently, the drinking of it the kind of experience now almost disappeared. Most Rhônes have a nice fragrance, and in color are so deep a red as to have occasionally a brownish tinge, a color tone most red wines acquire only with age. This tone, called *pelure d'oignon*, is plainly seen in the uneven ring a fine wine leaves on the sides of a glass after the liquid has swirled away. Also marked is a flinty dryness, one of their chief characteristics. The red Châteauneuf-du-Pape 1937 shows it handsomely.

In the past it has been necessary to warn against handling Rhônes carelessly, because of the heavy sediment they threw, but for the last ten years or so bottles have had little deposit, and I have felt after tasting that in each case the wine would have been bigger and richer if the deposit had not been removed at the time of the final bottling, as there seems little doubt it was. Drawing sediment from a wine is apt to arrest its development. Unfortunately the Rhônes are not the only wines so treated.

Rhône wines are best and most reliable when the name of the estate or Château where the wine is made is attached to the name of the district. Wines sold simply as Côtes-du-Rhône, Hermitage, or Châteauneuf-du-Pape may be pleasant but give no guarantee.

A part of the vineyard of Côte-Rôtie is subdivided into the *Côte-Brune* and the *Côte-Blonde*. The vines bearing red and white grapes are grown together in the vineyard, and the wine is made with one third white grapes and two thirds red, all pressed and fermented together. The *Brune* gives body to the wine, the *Blonde* finesse, the white grape called Viognier being largely responsible for the character so special to Côte-Rôtie.

The best red Hermitage is made by blending the wines of three sections of the hillside, Les Baissards for body, Les Gréffieux for finesse, Le Méal for flavor. Growers own vineyards, or portions of a vineyard, in each section. L'Ermite is a good red Hermitage, perhaps a little light.

Châteauneuf-du-Pape is a wine blended of four grape varieties in which Grenache predominates. The best-known growths are Château de la Nerthe, Clos St. Pierre, Clos des Papes, Domaine de Nallys, Châteaux des Fines-Roches, Fortia, Rayas, and La Bernardine.

WHITE RHÔNE WINES

The white wines of this region must not be overlooked. One rarely sees a white Châteauneuf-du-

Pape or Côte-Rôtie away from the Rhône district, but white Hermitage gets about considerably and is welcome wherever it goes. The Rhône whites are as delicious in their way as the reds, their bouquet fragrant and their flavor fine and dry. They need as much age as the reds.

The best white Hermitages are: Hermitage Blanc, *Tout Court*, Chante-Alouette, Les Beaumes, Les Rocoules, Les Murets.

Other good white Rhônes are Crozes Blanc and Tavel Blanc. And there is a pretty pink Tavel, called Tavel Rosé. Perhaps the best *rosé* wines come from Tavel, Arbois, and Anjou, but *rosé* wines are best enjoyed where they grow. They should be drunk young, at the peak of their freshness, last year's wine at the oldest. To be distinguished should never be required of them. Properly drunk, that is, young wines cooled and served in generous glasses for a summer lunch, they are fragrant, light, and pleasant. Most of the *rosé* wines coming to this country are shipped when too old, and they are pink all right but also punk, too often hard and sour.

VINTAGE YEARS IN RHÔNE WINES

The wines of 1937 and 1943 remain excellent and worth searching out. 1945, 1947, 1949, and 1950 produced splendid wines, and 1952 great ones. The '53's were less spectacular in Rhône than elsewhere. 1954

was a very good year, 1955 another great one; and
1956, 1957, and 1958 are rated fair, above average,
and good. The '59's are good, not distinguished.

∽ ∽

LOIRE WINES

The wines of another river valley, the Loire, are
chiefly white wines, lighter than those hitherto mentioned but with the power to maintain strength in
maturity belying their gaiety and lightness. A Vouvray of a great year, made properly and not tampered
with, may reach such an age as to make it seem age-
less. Vouvray, a wine of the Touraine, is not the only
great wine of the valley; La Coulée de Serrant from
Anjou is rated by experts as one of the great white
wines of France.

For purposes of separation and identification, the
Loire Valley may be divided into three sections:
Anjou, Touraine, and Nièvre.

The wines of Anjou, comprising those of the Côteaux de la Loire, Côteaux du Layon, Muscadet,
Saumur, and the Côteaux du Loir et de la Sarthe,
grown in a district where the climate is mild and
fairly even, are somewhat sweeter than those encountered up the river. This is not to suggest that they
resemble one another. They share only in inclining
toward the sweet rather than the dry, and in their
qualities of lightness and the charm of their bouquet.
A variety of vine stocks are grown in this area, and

the wines show considerable diversity. The Côteaux de la Loire produces the outstanding wines, although the Saumurs, when made by the Sauternes method and of a good year, age well and like to think of themselves as quite the equals of the great Sauternes, and the *vins* du Layon are lively and fragrant, sometimes having a slight natural sparkle. The lesser wines of the district, however, can be described as agreeable table wines only, refreshing when drunk young and on the spot. Muscadet is a light wine, palatable but not great. The same is true of the wines of Loir et Sarthe. When not too sweet the wines of Anjou make exceptionally good luncheon wines. They have a sunny quality that is nice.

The wines of Anjou, and also of Touraine, are often *pétillant,* a designation, as explained before, given to still wines that sparkle of their own accord. Early in the last century a M. Ackerman began making wines by the Champagne process, and now a considerable portion of the wines of Saumur are so treated. The Sparkling Saumurs undoubtedly lack the qualities that make Champagne great, but they do have the attractive traits native to Loire wines, and their worth is such as to insure them admirers on their own account. They are much to be preferred to inferior Champagnes.

The best-known growths of Anjou are the famous La Coulée de Serrant, La Roche-aux-Moines, and other vineyards of Château de Savennières in the Côteaux de la Loire; those of the parishes of Thouarcé (Bonnezeaux), Rochefort-sur-Loire (Quarts-de-Chaume), and Faye-, Beaulieu-, and Rablay-sur-Layon in the Côteaux du Layon; also Montsoreau, Bizet, and Brézé in Saumur.

Vouvray is sometimes dry and sometimes sweet, and sometimes both together; sometimes it has a natural sparkle, sometimes a manufactured sparkle, and sometimes it is still. At its poorest it is nothing; at its best it is made of the Pinot grape and is enchanting. In 1929, at the old Hotel de la Couronne, at Rouen, I tasted a Vouvray of the great year 1911. No other was ever found to compare with it, although a 1931 Vouvray from Rochecorbon, a clean and strictly natural wine, approached it in size if not in subtlety. The Rochecorbon was a trifle hard but very good.

The finest wines are grown at Vouvray and Rochecorbon. The vineyards are not large and the growths are few in number: Clos du Bourg, Clos de la Barre, Qui d'Amant, Clos Le Mont, l'Auberdière, Bouchet, Château de Moncontour in Vouvray; and Château Chevrier and Clos l'Olivier in Rochecorbon. The laws of delimitation in this district will work greatly to the advantage of the consumer seeking honest wines. The quantity is always small, and blending and adulteration have been the rule rather than the exception.

The best reds of the Loire are made in the Touraine, although the excellent Château Parney, grown near Saumur is, properly speaking, an Anjou. None has great merit but they can be delightful. Especially so are the light and fruity wines of Chinon and Borgueil, again recommended as luncheon wines. As with Vouvray, they can be drunk young with pleasure.

Far up the Valley of the Loire, approaching Nevers and not many miles west of the low hills of the Côte d'Or, is the town of Pouilly-sur-Loire, which produces Pouilly-Fumé, a pleasantly dry white wine. Pouilly-Fumé, as mentioned earlier, is frequently confused with Pouilly-Fuissé. The confusion is in name only, as one is made of the Sauvignon grape of Bordeaux, and the other of the white Pinot of Burgundy. Quincy lies just to the west.

Professor Saintsbury had no very high esteem of Loire wines, and I myself have observed that one's first enthusiasm for them tends to fade if one drinks them steadily for a time. They are like people who make a remarkable first impression, but, seen too often, disappoint us. Nevertheless, one of the pleasant things about a visit to Touraine and Anjou is the endless succession of little local wines found everywhere. Never to be forgotten is a sparkling Chenonceaux drunk under a grape arbor not far from the beautiful château, and a red wine at not more than fifty cents a bottle which astonished and delighted me when I found it at a humble eating-place in the crossroads hamlet of L'Ile-Bouchard, near Chinon. It had no name, but it was good.

The vintage years apply here only to the white

wines. The red wines should be drunk young. Fine wines were made in 1952, 1953, and especially in 1955; frost in 1956 and 1957 spared only fortunate sections; the 1958's were fair; the 1959's breaking all records.

∽ ∽

ALSACE WINES

The wines of Alsace and Lorraine are commonly grouped as Alsace or Alsatian wines, and are white. Before the first World War they went principally to Germany, sometimes for sale as German types but more often for blending purposes. Since the inclusion of the provinces into the Republic of France a great effort has been made to talk them up as competitors of German wines, which they somewhat resemble. This is unfortunate, as the Alsatian wines are not in the same class with the great Rhine wines and suffer by an unnecessary comparison. Actually they can stand very well on their own.

When young, Alsatian wines are likely to have an acid taste, like that of inferior Rhine wines, and since most of the wines are drunk too young, the impression has grown that this fault is characteristic of the wine. With proper age, that is, when they are at least three years old, the acid taste disappears and they are clean, well balanced, and have a nice follow-through. A bitter aftertaste is not typical. Sometimes they have the flowery quality of a good Moselle, and like the Moselles, they are especially suitable as lunch wines when seafood is served.

As in Germany, so in Alsace, the names of the different types of vine from which the wine is made figure prominently on labels. The best wines are generally made from the grapes called Riesling, Traminer, and Pinot Gris. Grapes of less reputation are Gentil, Sylvaner, Gewürztraminer, and Chasselas. After tasting the various types of Alsace wines quite extensively, it appears to me that the Traminer and Gewürztraminer are the best. Sylvaner is so dry and flinty that it hurts. Chasselas seems to have little distinction. Riesling is fine, with a nice bouquet, but often too dry for the ordinary taste. Gentil is a step up the ladder, quite dry, but nothing like so dry as Sylvaner. Traminer and especially Gewürztraminer, which is a lovely golden color and can have a fresh and delightful bouquet, are the least dry of the lot and make pleasurable drinking.

Often a wine will be labeled merely with one of the vine names. On labels of the better wines, however, the vine name is connected with the local district name, coming sometimes before it and sometimes after, as, for instance, Riesling de Riquewihr or Riquewihr-Riesling. It is therefore well to remember the principal vine names and the place names.

Of the latter, Turckheim, Colmar, Eguisheim, Riquewihr, Kayserberg, Ribeauvillé, Ammerschwihr, Zellenberg, Guebwiller, Mittelwihr, Wintzenheim, and Thann; also Molsheim, Barr, Gertwiller, Epfig,

Wolxheim, and Obernai (Clos Sainte-Odile) are recommended.

As to vintages here, 1952 and 1953 produced great wines, and 1955, 1957, 1958 good, occasionally very good ones. The 1959's should be charmers, heavy with natural sweetness.

∽ ∽

OTHER FRENCH WINES

The whole of France is a vineyard, to a point in the north, that is, where grapes will not ripen and distillation begins in earnest. All a chapter on French wines can do is touch the high spots, omitting the many hundreds of "small" wines, some of them very good, that are designed for local consumption and give such unexpected pleasure to the stranger who comes on them in carafe in small country inns.

Between the small and the great are various districts producing fine wines, wines seldom seen in this country but worth the trouble, in France, to hunt out.

JURA WINES

Before the French Revolution the Jura was one of the very important wine regions in France, having extensive vineyards owned by religious orders and prominent families. The wine industry, however, never recovered from the breaking up of the vineyards after the Revolution, and the phylloxera, and at the present time only a small quantity of wine is made and that quantity is difficult to find.

The district produces wines of all shades and kinds, red, *rosé*, sparkling, yellow, and white, and they are considered, especially the yellow and white varieties, because their novelty gives them a certain interest. The yeast-ferments on the skin of the grapes are very like those of the Sherry grape, and both wines are fermented in cask in a similar manner—that is, in open casks, with the wine protected from harmful elements only by its own *flor*. The wines of the Jura mature in cask longer than any other wine made to-day, sometimes resting quietly for as long as twenty years. After bottling they live to a great age, remaining pungent and like no other wine in the world.

The best growths are Arbois, which produces both red and white wines, L'Étoile, and Château-Châlon, the wine on which Pasteur worked when he made his momentous discovery. In 1934 I picked up a bottle of Château-Châlon 1870 at Gosling's in Bermuda. I was immensely interested in the wine because of its rarity and the age of this particular bottle. It was dark amber in color and had a bouquet like the scent of olives. It was dry but not sour in taste and had a hint of flavor like that of a very light Sherry or Madeira—odd and completely individual.

SAVOY

Both red and white wines are grown on the upper Rhône in Savoy. The best known of them is Seyssel, which in its white variety is said to be an excellent dry wine, in sunny years taking on a degree of sweetness. It is often slightly sparkling and is another excellent luncheon wine.

MONBAZILLAC

A white wine grown just to the north and outside the delimitation of Bordeaux. The wine is made by the Sauternes method and, when properly aged and of a good year, is a close rival to a fine Sauternes, although quite unlike it in fragrance and body. It should be drunk with dessert only.

BÉARN

Jurançon, famous wine of the western Pyrenees, is noted for its deep golden color, good body, rich and acceptable sweetness, and charming bouquet. There are many vineyards, not all producing wines of equal quality. Research in these wines must be done at Biarritz and Pau, as they seldom stray far outside their home territory.

∽ ∽

BRANDY

Ordinary Brandy, taken with charged water, making Brandy and Soda or Brandy highball, is still a great favorite with Englishmen. It used to be so drunk in America, but it lost ground after the destruction by the phylloxera, when the shortage of

Brandy put gin and whiskies into the social register, so to speak, where they remained even after Brandy became available again. Now the taste in general is for very fine old Brandies, which are taken as a liqueur with after-dinner coffee—a *chasse-café*, the old-time British called it. It should be served in a very large balloon glass of thin clear crystal. An extremely small amount of Brandy, standing in the bottom of the glass, may be rotated within the glass, which is warmed with the palms of the hands to bring out the rich, incisive fragrance. The glass is somewhat contracted at the top, forming a large air chamber in which the aroma may circulate beneath the nose. One should enjoy this aroma to the full and drink the Brandy in little sips. It is helpful to the digestion.

The finest Brandy is that of the Charente district of Cognac, and is made only in the years when climatic conditions are right for the proper ripening of the grapes. It is distilled, paradoxically, from white wines that give no pleasure when drunk for themselves. The first distillate is made by the growers, then sold to the merchants who redistill and in other ways prepare the product for its eventual sale. Cognac ages in the wood and does not improve in bottle; hence the length of time it remains in cask is important.

Bottles labeled "Napoleon" Brandy used to be seen about. They never were anything but an absurdity, designed to rook the innocent. I have tasted fairish

Brandy from bottles labeled "Napoleon 1848"—which I suppose refers to the last Napoleon, though what he had to do with this Brandy it would be difficult to ascertain—and in no case was it either natural uncolored Brandy, pure Brandy, or Brandy more than twenty or twenty-five years old. "Napoleon" Brandy is in the class with Sparkling Burgundy. May the devil take both, and the people who put them out.

A pure, uncolored Cognac of great age is extremely difficult to find, even in France. The truth is that a Brandy which is not sweetened and artificially colored is today a rare exception in the trade, though possibly this is not so true of Brandies that are frankly young and hot as it is of those pretending to a fair age.

Ask a straightforward dealer in the United States, England, or France why this is, and he will tell you that it is because pure Brandy, except when very old, no longer suits the public taste, and also because the public likes its Brandy brown in color rather than pale.

But who taught the public to like it that way? Did the public ask to have caramel syrup added to its Brandy? I don't believe so. I think the distillers discovered that by sweetening their Brandy they could achieve a sort of smoothness resembling the smoothness that, in a connoisseur's Brandy, is achieved by aging in the wood.

If you are doubtful of a Brandy, a good test is this: Pour a small amount of the Brandy into a glass and add perhaps half a tumbler of boiling water. Then note the color and the smell. If the color is clear and the smell clean and spirituous there is nothing wrong. I have seen Brandy of a widely known mark which under this test becomes slightly cloudy and develops an unpleasant stink. It would indeed take one of Dr. Johnson's "heroes" to drink such stuff.

The same test is a good one to apply to whisky and particularly to gin. I have never tried it on a doubtful Burgundy, but I should think that it would work.

Certain Spanish Brandies are excellent, especially when aged. They are lighter than French Brandies and have a distinct clean flavor of their own. Even cheap Brandies tasted at little Spanish inns of no pretensions have been surprisingly light and smooth.

Portuguese Brandies are deeper in color and not so dry as French Brandies.

Types of French Brandy other than Cognac will be found listed in the table of Brandy designations which follows.

BRANDY DESIGNATIONS

COGNAC—The name Cognac may be applied only to Brandy distilled from a wine made of grapes grown within the legally defined district of Cognac, in Charente and Charente Inférieure, and must, by law, have not less than 30% alcohol (60 proof) and not more than 72% (144 proof). *Esprit de Cognac* may have between 76% (152 proof) and 85% (170 proof).

The finest Cognac is made of grapes from the inner circle of the area, or Première Zone, consisting of the famous districts of Grande Champagne, Petite Champagne, Borderies, and Fins Bois.

Distinctive Cognac marks are:

FINE CHAMPAGNE—supposedly an old and fine Brandy that by law must come from Grande Champagne or Petite Champagne.

GRANDE CHAMPAGNE—older and more choice than Fine Champagne.

GRANDE FINE CHAMPAGNE—just a little more so. A vintage of 1858 was so rich and full that the fragrance remained in the glass when left in the room overnight. The use of the word "Champagne" in connection with a wine and also with a Brandy puzzles many persons. As applied to Cognac Brandy the name is derived from the ancient name of the district which was called Champagne.

ARMAGNAC—A Brandy esteemed by the French second only to the Brandy of Cognac. It is made in the foothills of the Pyrenees, and when old can be better than the average Cognac, and more often tastes clean and straight.

MARC—A Brandy of curious medicinal flavor, distilled from the stems, skins, seeds, and other residue of grapes from which wine has already been pressed. It is made in Burgundy and in the Rhône district.

CALVADOS—Apple-Brandy from Normandy, the like of which few American applejack-drinkers ever encounter. It is aged in wood, like other Brandies, and gets a dark color from the barrel. Old Calvados is a pretty good liqueur, but very strong.

THE SIGNIFICANCE OF
CERTAIN CABALISTIC SIGNS

It is said that 1811 being a comet year a star was placed
on the bottles of brandy of that year. In 1812 two stars
appeared. In this manner this form of marking originated.

—F. GRAY GRISWOLD
(*French Wines and Havana Cigars*)

SIGNIFICANCE OF MARKS

Referring to the above, and the confusion of stars resulting, it must be said that their appearance does not
imply a standard of aging or of quality. They are used
on the bottles of almost all the better-known Cognac
firms to indicate the most popular of their special dis-
tillations. The age of the spirit so starred is determined
by the individual house, and may be from three years to
twenty.

Initials are a more reliable guarantee of quality:

> V.O.—Very Old
> V.S.E.P.—Very Superior Extra Pale
> V.S.O.P.—Very Superior Old Pale
> V.V.S.O.P.—More of the same
> X., or X.O.—Extra, or Extra Old

In addition, each house has special names to mark
their supreme products, among them Family Reserve,
Louis XIII, Napoleon, Bras d'Or, Cordon Bleu, Argent,
Anniversaire, and Triomphe.

Unless a Brandy is stamped *Nature, Nature Fine,* or *Cognac Nature,* it will be a blend.

A pleasant story going the rounds of the trade some time ago told of a woman newly employed in a wine-shop who, on being asked the meaning of the initials V.V.S.O.P., thought fast and said: "Very Very Swell Old Prandy."

CHAPTER FOUR

THE WINES OF GERMANY

Hocks, too, have compassed age. I have tasted senior Hocks. Their flavors are as a brook of many voices; they have depth, also. —GEORGE MEREDITH
(*The Egoist*)

The supreme wine-producing district of Germany is the Rheingau, on the right bank of the Rhine. Opposite, on the left bank, lies Rheinhesse, also an extremely important district, and, adjoining Rheinhesse, the Bavarian Palatinate dips down to the oft-sung river. The valley of the Nahe and the valleys of the Moselle and its tributaries the Saar and the Ruwer are also rich in vineyards, while in the region of Würzburg, famous for its beer, in the district called Franconia, Stein wines are produced.

The principal wines of Germany are white. The types are multiple but the best of them have in common a very charming characteristic: a fresh, flowery bouquet. Many experts rate the German wines as pre-eminent among the white wines of the world. Possibly. Certainly the best are gorgeous and they are tremendous, and drinking some of them leaves one wordless, with only a cheer. But unfortunately the big beauties are relatively few in number and they are costly. And when it comes to the district wines, or those made in ordinary or off years, the buyer must be spry in order not to find himself with wines that are light, thin, or even sour. Which isn't to say that spryness in this case does not pay—it does. To find a "small" Rhine or Moselle, lively and good, and bought at a price that permits it to be drunk frequently and enjoyed, is worth another cheer.

Climatic conditions place natural limits, and a number of hazards, in the way of wine-growing in Germany, and probably because of this, the art of viniculture is more highly developed there than elsewhere. Certainly no wine region of the limited proportions of the German produces wines of greater or more subtle diversity. Most of the large vineyards are broken up into a number of small holdings varying in size from a few rows of vines to larger sections, and the many proprietors pick their grapes and make their wine by methods entirely individual. In vineyards where it is possible to make great wines, the grapes are picked in the most exact manner as to the time of picking and selection of grapes, and it is general practice to crush each day's picking and mark the filled cask with a number to differentiate the wine made on that day from those made on succeeding days, each of which will be unlike the others in taste and quality. The marks, both of picking and crushing, are transferred to the label when the wine is bottled, with the result that no wine in the world identifies itself more completely by the information carried on the label than the German. Moreover, the laws governing the wine industry are well devised and rigorous. Estate-bottling is widespread, and great efforts are made to protect the consumer from fraud.

The nomenclature of German wines is complicated and there is no short cut to learning the terms if one wants to buy the wines wisely. The labels appear to be hopeless riddles, but one soon learns to notice terms—or the absence of terms—that tell so plainly what one can expect from the wine.

A district wine must, by law, contain not less than 51% of the wine of the district. Thus a wine labelled Niersteiner and giving no further information, is a blend: At least 51% is grown in an unnamed vineyard —or vineyards—of Nierstein, and the remainder is anyone's guess. The district wines cannot be dismissed, however. Because of the immense amount of time and labor expended in the making of the great wines, they are always expensive. As a consequence the average cellar is likely to have many more district than big vineyard names. A wine worth buying will show a date, and the shipper's name is important. A more reliable wine is one that has a vineyard name attached, as for instance, Niersteiner Domtal or Forster Altenberg. It costs a bit more but is worth it. The name of the vineyard where the wine was grown gives it an authenticity the purely district wine lacks.

A fine German wine, guaranteed by law to be as described, should bear on its label some or all of the following: (1) the year of vintage, (2) the name of the district whence it comes, (3) the name of the vineyard in that district, (4) the name of the species of vine from which the grapes were grown, (5) a term indicating the degree of ripeness of the grapes when picked, (6) the name of the grower or shipper, and (7) preceding the name of the grower or shipper, one of the following words: *"Wachstum," "Creszenz," "Gewächs,"* (meaning either the property of, or the growth of), *"Natur"* or *"Naturrein,"* signifying that the wine is unsugared. A more powerful guarantee, not only against sugaring but also against blending, are the words: *"Originalabfüllung," "Originalabzug," "Kellerabfüllung," "Kellerabzug,"* or *"Schlossabzug,"* various ways of saying that the wine was bottled by the owner—on his property, in his cellar, or at his schloss.

The terms indicating the degree of ripeness of the grapes when picked are:

Auslese—a wine made from selected bunches of fully ripened grapes. The gradation of fineness rises from *Auslese* to *Feine Auslese*, to *Hochfeine*, and to *Feinste Auslese* at the top. An *Auslese* should be the driest of German wines.

Beeren Auslese—a wine made from selected single grapes cut from the selected bunches. *Golden-beerenauslese* and *Edelbeerenauslese* signify special selection of single berries. These can be luscious and beautiful wines, with just a shade of sweetness and a lovely bouquet.

Spätlese—a wine from grapes gathered late in their period of ripening. They are delicious and fragrant, and on the sweet side. In fine years and with age, they can be perfect dessert wines.

Trockenbeeren Auslese—a wine made from grapes allowed to hang until almost dry. The wines are honey-sweet, and they have a flavor and bouquet as good as, and sometimes surpassing in magnificence, those of a great Yquem. They are made only in exceptional years and at estates able to afford both the costly gamble of leaving the grapes to ripen to the extent they must and the skilled staff required for their making. The volume is always small and the wines sell at incredibly high prices. Single bottles of the great year 1921 fetched around seventy dollars and even more when sold at auction in Berlin.

Included here is a copy of a label showing how the terms explained above reveal the type and quality of a wine:

Fass. Nr. 16   Rheingau
1934er
Rüdesheimer Klosterkiesel
Riesling Spätlese

Kellerabfüllung aus der Gutskellerei des
Grafen von Francken Sierstorpff
vorm. Freiherrn von Stumm-Halberg
Rüdesheim im Rheingau

All of which means a big (Rheingau) and fairly sweet (Spätlese) wine of a fine year, from the Klosterkiesel vineyard in the district of Rüdesheim, drawn from a numbered cask and bottled in the cellar of the estate. The wine is described in a cellar-book as a "big slashing Rhine." The word "slashing" is hardly the one I normally would choose to describe a wine, but its use illustrates the statement above that in the presence of some of these wines one is wordless. In this case there seemed to be no proper word and "slashing" had to do. The wine had everything.

The designations as to sweet and dry may be relied upon in the main, although occasionally one has surprises. I have several times come on astonishingly sweet Ausleses, and Spätleses too dry for pleasant drinking. This irregularity is accounted for by the northerly position of the vineyards and the fact that here, as in France, wines of varying quality come from the same vineyard, the fineness of the wine depending upon conditions, climatic and otherwise, in various parts of the vineyard. Also, in years of uncommon warmth, the selected bunches of the first picking are full and rich, and a sharp turn in the autumn weather can cut the sweetness of a Spätlese by several degrees. In bad years, when the wine proves hopelessly inferior, the great German vineyards sell it immediately as common wine. The temptation to add sugar is the greatest in the years when the wines need only a small push to make them of an accepted type. The laws that have reduced the practice are to be applauded. Better a dry Spätlese than one all doped up.

The great Rhines are not as useful as the dry white Burgundies for table use, for though fine German wines are in themselves magnificent, they are maladjusted to most foods. They are often too sweet. Only a rich and fairly dry Auslese or a Cabinet wine is sufficiently forceful to stand up to meat or fowl, and the lighter Moselles are better with fish. On the other hand, unless one is especially fortunate in a Spätlese or is drinking the scarce and expensive Trockenbeeren Auslese, they are not sweet enough to be out-and-out dessert wines like the honeyed Bordeaux. They are at their best at odd hours it seems to me—as eleven o'clock wines, whether eleven in the morning or eleven in the evening, and five o'clock wines, served with biscuits or with a light supper. The most perfect Jesuitengarten I ever tasted, an Auslese of 1921, was served at eleven in the morning with caviar and dry biscuits. The Germans themselves often serve their big wines at these convivial hours, an especially pleasant act of hospitality; and they often appear at five o'clock instead of coffee or tea, the accompanying biscuit a dry thing, very like a shortbread.

The lighter-bodied Moselles and the lesser Rhines are easier to place. They are ideal with fish, especially the milder-flavored varieties such as lobster and scallops, and they are good with light summer lunches or with chicken sandwiches on a picnic. Nothing is nicer with a sweet Moselle than fruit—a ripe peach is perfect—and the light sweetness of an unpretentious Rhine admirably suits such dishes as tongue with Madeira sauce and *poulet-a-la-crême* with Sherry.

When drinking the equivalent of *vins ordinaires,* cool the wines even to icing. Icing will remove all that is poor in the flavor and often make them delicious.

The bottles used for German wines are tall and slender and distinctive as to color. The wines of the three Rhine districts are drawn off into brown bottles; those of the Moselle, the Saar, and the Ruwer, in green bottles.

∽ ∽

RHEINGAU

From the Rheingau district, which begins opposite the town of Bingen and continues to just north of Mainz, a district less than twenty-two kilometers long and seven wide, come the greatest wines—wines described by a French authority as "second to none in the world in point of excellence," and by an English authority as "unexcelled as they are inimitable."

The Rheingau wines are bigger and have more power and a greater volume of bouquet than other wines of the Rhine. As a general rule, all German wines should be drunk fairly young, even these, the greatest of them. They are at their best in three, five, and up to eight years, but they can be drunk much younger—and much older. A Johannisberger Kerzenstück 1933 was delicious and ready to drink at nine to ten months old; and the wines of a great year, especially the sweeter varieties, go on for ten or fifteen or more years. Two great 1934's, a Rüdesheimer Schlossberg Auslese and a Dürkheimer Hochbenn Auslese, opened in the spring of 1956, were soft, fruity, and beautiful. They showed no sign of excessive age.

The vineyards producing the finest wines are those of Schloss Johannisberg, Marcobrunn, and Steinberg. Schloss Reinhartshausener Cabinet is another aristocrat among wines. The hillsides of Johannisberg and Rüdesheim were the first planted by order of the great Charlemagne after he had observed that the snow, then covering the countryside, disappeared more quickly from their slopes than from other less well exposed hills in the neighborhood. The first vines planted, brought from France, have long since been replaced, and only the Riesling makes the glorious wines of Johannisberg. The famous Cabinet wines from this vineyard with their mauve, white, and lilac seals, each representing its own degree of excellence, are produced as late in the season as weather permits, and they have great power. Other good wines made near by are Johannisbergers Erntebringer and Hölle.

Many of the vineyards in the Rheingau make wines that are only a little less fine than those of the great estates. As one thinks of the vineyards dotting the landscape from one big bend in the Rhine to the other, the mind's eye shifts from outdoor to indoor scenery, and settles on attractively set tables, pleasant company, and wines, some of them memorable. Noted in the cellar-books are a number of vineyards of Rüdesheim: Berg, Roseneck, Hinterhaus, Oberfeld, Klosterkiesel, Schlossberg, and several district Rüdesheimers. Most of the wines, tasted not once but repeatedly, were Ausleses or Spätleses, and while the record shows that the Rüdesheimers may lack something of the pronounced character noted in other wines of the Rheingau, many had charm and several were great, among them my "slashing" Klosterkiesel. The district Rüdesheimers were pleasant small wines, all shipped by the reliable firm of J. Langenbach & Sohne.

There are records of a number of Johannisbergers in addition to those mentioned above—a Kerzenstück was one of the treasures of my cellar, and the Kahlenbergs and a Claus Johannisberger were delicious wines. Among the Oestrichers, a Rheingarten was especially nice and I liked also the Deez. A Hallgarten Schönhell 1921 was an experience, as were most of the wines of that great year; and the list could go on through Rauenthalers, Geisenheimers, Hochheimers, Winkelers, and Erbachers, not all great wines by any means, but they were well selected, and whether simple or fine, they never failed to give their full measure of enjoyment.

The district of Hochheim, from which the British derived the abbreviation "Hock," their generic term for all Rhine wines, lies a little apart from this area but is always included in the Rheingau grouping.

Mention should be made of the best-known German red wine, that of Assmannshäuser, which is grown in the Rheingau. Its vine, called Spätburgunder, is an acclimatization of the Pinot vine, from which the great red Burgundies of the Côte d'Or are produced. Thomas Beer once told me that this wine has special affinity for Long Island duck, and there's something to be said for it. It's a rather thin red wine with a flavor of its own, lacking in any great body or distinction, but very good with tame duck.

RHEINHESSEN

The wines of the Rheingau dominate the Rhine picture and tend to blot out, or at least obscure, the very good wines of the other two districts, Rheinhesse and the Palatinate. This is unfortunate, because while the general run of Rheinhessen and Pfalz wines can be said to be softer, less rich, and less powerful than its counterpart in the Rheingau, certain wines in each district are outstandingly good. And there is the question of price. The demand in the market is primarily for Rheingaus and as a consequence the wines of the two lesser districts are not so expensive, making a search for good bottles well worth the trouble.

The grape from which all of the fine wines of the Rhine regions are made is the Riesling. While it is planted almost exclusively in the Rheingau, the same cannot be said of the Rheinhesse and the Palatinate, and the guarantee of the Riesling grape is necessary if one wants the best wines of either district. The Oestreicher, chief of the secondary plantings, can make a pleasant enough wine but one seldom having any claim to distinction.

Wines of the subdistricts of Nierstein and Oppenheim are considered the best of the Rheinhesse product and are known all over the world. Many of the vineyards of Nierstein and Oppenheim are planted to the Riesling grape, and some of their wines in great years are remarkable. The Rhine-wine listing at the Hotel St. Regis was topped off with a Niersteiner Pettental, Beeren Auslese 1934. It was a great big luscious beauty of a wine, sweet and round and full.

The most famous wine of the region is Liebfraumilch, which in former days came only from the Liebfrauenstift vineyard surrounding the Liebfrau Church at Worms. Latterly the name, being, because of its peculiarity, a good trade name, has been used as a blanket designation for all manner of Rhine wines, including some pretty sour ones. No one knows what Liebfraumilch should taste like until he has met Liebfrauen Stiftswein. Rieslings are planted in the vineyard at the church, and wine-making methods have always been of the best. The wine is perhaps not the greatest in the world, but a tasting-record well describes them as "beautiful, full, rather sweet, with a fine bouquet."

A fairish red wine is made at Ober-Ingelheim, the site of the castle from which Charlemagne had such clear view to the sunny slopes across the Rhine.

The wines of the Rheinhesse should be drunk while young and fresh.

∾ ∾

NAHE

The valley of the River Nahe, a tributary joining the Rhine at Bingen, is covered with vineyards producing wines we now must reckon with. Having been contented for centuries to make ordinary wines, the growers of the district, encouraged by the Provincial Wine School at Kreuznach, have methodically been tearing out the Oestreicher and other inferior grapes and replacing them with the Riesling. The result has been a number of new and surprisingly lovely wines, not Rhines, not Moselles, but with a touch of both. The principal district is Kreuznach.

∾ ∾

PALATINATE (PFALZ WINES)

The Palatinate is the largest of the German wine-producing districts and the most southern of the Rhine group. The comparatively warm summers give the wines a greater natural sweetness than one finds in the other Rhine wines, generally speaking, and it is possible to make Beeren Ausleses and Trockenbeeren Ausleses much more frequently here than elsewhere. Pfalz wines have a nice forthright quality that makes them greatly liked, although they lack the elegance and the clean dimensions of the Rheingaus. Also, secondary grapes are widely planted in this district, not only the Oestreicher, but the Traminer as well, and the more ordinary wines produced by these grapes tend to bring the general average down to the medium.

There are splendid wines to be found in the Palatinate, however. In about 1935 a small book of mine, *The Need of Change*, was translated into German, and since no payment could be made, due to the blocking of the mark, I suggested to the translator that he make a token return of a case or two of wine, and instructed him to consult Herr Walterspiel of the Four Seasons in Munich as to their selection. Two cases came, both Pfalz and both very near to perfection. One, a Forster Ungeheur 1934, the lighter of the two, was delicate and exquisite to the last drop, having not the faintest shadow of sharpness in its taste; the other, a Ruppertsberger Spiess Spätlese 1934, was a bigger wine than the Forster, but equally fine, being a kind of superb golden honey. The wines, served only to those who could appreciate them, lasted until 1944 and improved steadily, showing, right up to the end, no hint of weakness.

Other Pfalz wines noted as greatly liked were two Deidesheimers, a Grain, and a Leinhöle, both, contrary to all advice, which is to drink the Pfalz wines young, beautiful wines in beautiful condition at a fair age. And all of the Forsters tasted were admirable wines. They have very particular characteristics, which, once known and appreciated, are never forgotten. Besides the Spiess, several of the Ruppertsbergers, a Hoheburg, and a Helbig, were thoroughly nice wines and a Dürkheimer Hochbenn was clean and lovely, with a delicate bouquet.

∽ ∽

MOSELLE

The vineyards of the Moselle, terraced like giant steps cut into the hillsides, date from the second century and are the oldest in Germany. By strange and lucky chance, probably having something to do with soil, the phylloxera pest skipped the valley entirely, and the good roots of the Riesling grape to which the valley is planted are German and not American.

To try to describe a wine in words always is a temptation, one to which most of us succumb, but in all my tries I have succeeded but once in getting onto paper something I liked. It was a heading for a listing of Moselle for a wine-card: "A typical Moselle will have a subtle dryness along with a flowery bouquet, and a light frivolous quality, like a Strauss waltz played in a garden."

As noted earlier, Moselles have a tendency, especially in the spring, to be gently sparkling. It's an enchanting quality. At other times, without the sparkle, they have something of the flavor of a very light still Champagne. They mature early and continue beyond their short lives only when especially fine or when of the sweeter and stouter Spätlese or Beeren Auslese varieties. There are records in the cellar-books of Moselles remaining young and being pleasantly drinkable at twelve and fifteen years of age, but they seldom are so obliging and, generally speaking, they should be drunk before their fifth year. Indeed, I think it is not too much to say that unless the buyer knows, or can learn, all about the shipper, and the wine is of a good year, none but wines of a very recent year should be bought. The variation in quality is rather wide, and careful selection is important. Year-old Moselles may be delicious.

From the point of view of the excellence of its wines, the valley of the Moselle is divided into Lower, Middle, and Upper, the Lower beginning at the town of Coblenz. The finest wines come from the vineyards of the Middle section, although the wines of Enkircher can be good, and I noted a Pündericher Staaden as being delightful.

The Middle Moselle is one long succession of vineyards producing capital wines, the best-known being those of Erden, Uerzig, Zeltingen, Wehlen, Graach, Berncastel, Brauneberg, Josephshöf, Piesport, and Dhron. Wines from all, and from others as well, provided me with much pleasure from time to time, among them Piesporter Goldtröpfchen, which never failed to be fine; Uerziger Würzgarten, a stand-by in the household and never disappointing; Josephshöfer, in a class of its own; several Braunebergers, which were extremely pleasant; a Graacher Münzlay, beautifully keeping its strength and vigor into its tenth year; and as a magnificent climax, a Berncasteler Doctor 1921, Trockenbeeren Auslese #24, which was the greatest German wine I ever tasted. The color was that of Madeira, and the bouquet and flavor were of a dimension I had never before encountered. In the matter of sweet wines the comparison is always to an Yquem, and on this occasion the lovely French lady was left far behind.

The vineyard producing Berncasteler Doctor is undoubtedly the most famous of the district, and it owes its sudden rise to fame in the 1890's to Edward VII. Edward, as Prince and King, amply demonstrated that he knew his wines and believed in good living. It was he who started the public dining in England which reached its height of elegance in the

Sunday-night dinners given at the Carlton Hotel when M. Escoffier was chef.

There are a number of Berncasteler Doctors on the market, and the only way to get a good one is to refuse all but the Thanisch growths and pay the price.

The Upper Moselle produces few wines that could be considered outstanding, the best of the region coming from the tributary valleys of the Saar and the Ruwer.

〜 〜

THE SAAR AND THE RUWER

The vineyards of the Saar and the Ruwer produce wines so like the Moselles that it is sometimes difficult to distinguish between them. Many connoisseurs prefer the Saar wines to all but the best of the Moselles, with certain growths of the Ruwer included in top listing. The greater acidity of Saar wines may account for part of the preference—it gives them a brisk quality the Moselles sometimes lack. Acidity is responsible also for the warning issued by several of the experts that Saar and Ruwer wines are safely bought only in good years.

The best wines come from Canzem, Ockfen, Oberemel, Wiltingen, and Scharzhof. The wines of Scharzhof, Scharzberger, and Scharzhofberger are unequaled when the weather has been right, very often excelling all of the wines of the Moselle.

The Ruwer valley adds several familiar names to the list of the Saar: Eitelsbach, Maximin Grünhäus, and Casel. All show a flinty quality which is one of the hallmarks of the wines of this region.

～ ～

STEINWEIN

Although this Bavarian wine grew in popularity and favor in the years before the last war, neither became so great as the wine deserves. It is full-bodied in the way that a white Burgundy is full-bodied, and indeed, a good Würzburger Stein often seems to be a fine white Burgundy speaking with a strong German accent. They are very satisfying wines, with a nice depth of flavor and the bouquet characteristic of most German wines. They keep longer than any other wine of Germany, improving steadily in the picturesque squat bottle, called *Boxbeutel,* or *Bocksbeutel,* by which name the wine itself is often called. Steinwein takes high rank among German wines, and one feels well repaid for the time spent in hunting good ones.

VINTAGE YEARS

The German wine districts have had two outstanding pairs of years: 1949-1950 and 1952-1953. 1949 was one of the greatest years on record, its wines along with the '53's and the '59's being compared to the 1921's of blessed memory. Excellent wines were made in 1952, a shade less fine than the '53's, but the '54's were a failure. The '55's were hit by frost, and the same hazard devastated the vineyards in 1956. Although volume, for the same reason, was cut sharply in 1957, better than average wines were made. The wines of 1958 were good, and those of 1959 should be tremendous.

Moselle wines are bottled young for early drinking, so, except for the finest, the fact that 1950, 1953, and 1955 were especially fortunate years in this district is almost entirely for the record. The enchanting 1959's we should be drinking soon.

THE WINES OF GERMANY

In this classification the first name is usually that of the district, and the second that of the vineyard. Exceptions are marked with asterisk.

RHEINGAU

Rüdesheimer Berg	Rüdesheimer Klosterkiesel
Rüdesheimer Berg Burgweg	Geisenheimer Rothenberg
Rüdesheimer Berg Schlossberg	Geisenheimer Klauserweg
	Geisenheimer Morschberg
Rüdesheimer Berg Roseneck	Geisenheimer Katzenloch
	*Schloss Johannisberger
Rüdesheimer Berg Zollhaus	Johannisberger Erntebringer
Rüdesheimer Bischofsberg	
Rüdesheimer Oberfeld	Johannisberger Kerzenstück
Rüdesheimer Hinterhaus	Johannisberger Vogelsang

RHEINGAU—*continued*

Johannisberger Hölle
Johannisberger Kahlenberg
*Schloss Vollradser
Winkeler Dachsberg
Winkeler Steinacker
Winkeler Honigberg
Mittelheimer Bangert
Mittelheimer
  Magdalenenacker
Hallgartener Schönhell
Hallgartener Deitelsberg
Oestricher Doosberg
Oestricher Deez
Oestricher Lenchen
Oestricher Eiserweg
Oestricher Rheingarten
Hattenheimer Nussbrunnen
Hattenheimer
  Engelmannsberg

Hattenheimer
  Wisselbrunnen
*Steinberger
*Schloss Rheinhartshausener
*Marcobrunner or Erbacher
  Marcobrunn
Erbacher Hohenrain
Erbacher Honigberg
Erbacher Katz
Eltviller Sonnenberg
Kiedricher Gräfenburg
Kiedricher Sandgrub
Rauenthaler Steinnacher
Rauenthaler Burggraben
Rauenthaler Wagenkehr
Rauenthaler Berg
Hochheimer Daubhaus
Hochheimer Kirchenstück
Hochheimer Domdechaney

RHEINHESSEN

Binger Rosengarten
Binger Scharlachberg
Binger Eiselberg
Binger Schlossberg
Binger Schwätzerchen
Büdesheimer Scharlachberg
Laubenheimer Berg
Laubenheimer Edelmann
Laubenheimer Neuberg

Laubenheimer Heide
Bodenheimer Kahlenberg
Bodenheimer Burgweg
Bodenheimer Neuberg
Nackenheimer Rothenberg
Nackenheimer Fritzenhöll
Nackenheimer Stiel
Niersteiner Domtal
Niersteiner Auflangen

RHEINHESSEN—*continued*

Niersteiner Pettental
Niersteiner Hipping
Niersteiner Findling
Niersteiner Rehbach
Niersteiner Glöck
Oppenheimer Goldberg

Oppenheimer Sackträger
Oppenheimer Kreuz
Oppenheimer Zuckerberg
Oppenheimer Schlossberg
Liebfrauen Stiftswein, or
  Kirchenstück

PALATINATE (PFALZ WINE)

Kallstädter Kronenberg
Dürkheimer Hochbenn
Dürkheimer Schenkenböhl
Dürkheimer Klosterberg
Dürkheimer Steinberg
Wachenheimer Böhlig
Wachenheimer Gerümpel
Wachenheimer Wolfsdarm
Wachenheimer
  Fuchsmantel
Forster Jesuitengarten
Forster Altenberg
Forster Ungeheuer
Forster Kirchenstück
Forster Langenböhl

Deidesheimer Grain
Deidesheimer Leinhöhle
Deidesheimer Kieselberg
Deidesheimer Hofstück
Deidesheimer
  Herrgottsacker
Ruppertsberger Helbig
Ruppertsberger Hofstück
Ruppertsberger Hoheburg
Ruppertsberger Spiess
Königsbacher Idig
Königsbacher Erbenbrecht
Haardter Schlossberg
Mussbacher Hundertmorgen
Mussbacher Spiegel

NAHE

Kreuznacher Kronenberg
Kreuznacher Narrenkappe
Schloss Böckelheimer
  Kupfergrube

Schloss Böckelheimer
  Mühlberg

MOSELLE

Pündericher Staaden
Enkircher Montaneubel
Enkircher Steffensberg
Trabener Würzgarten
Trabener Schlossberg
Trabener Kräuterhaus
Trarbacher Halsberg
Trarbacher Hühneberg
Cröver Niederberg
Cröver Kuhkehr
Cröver Steffensberg
Erdener Treppchen
Erdener Prälat
Erdener Herzlay
Erdener Herrenberg
Uerziger Schwarzlay
Uerziger Würzgarten
Zeltinger Sonnenuhr
Zeltinger Himmelreich
Zeltinger Schlossberg
Wehlener Sonnenuhr
Wehlener Feinter
Wehlener Rothlay
Wehlener Nonnenlay

Graacher Himmelreich
Graacher Domprobst
Graacher Abtie
Graacher Münzlay
Berncasteler Doctor
Berncasteler Pfaffenberg
Berncasteler Badstube
Berncasteler Schwan
Berncasteler Lay
Berncasteler Rosenberg
Brauneberger Juffer
Brauneberger Kammer
Brauneberger Falkenberg
Dhroner Roterd
Dhroner Hofberg
Dhroner Kandel
*Josephshöfer
Piesporter Goldtröpfchen
Piesporter Günterslay
Piesporter Falkenberg
Piesporter Wehr
Neumagener Rosengartchen
Trittenheimer Falkenberg
Trittenheimer Neuberg

SAAR

Filzener Pulchen
Filzener Herrenberg
Canzemer Berg
Canzemer Sonnenberg

Canzemer Altenberg
Wiltinger Kupp
Wiltinger Braune Kupp
Wiltinger Braunfels

SAAR—*continued*

Wiltinger Schlossberg
Wiltinger Gottesfuss
Scharzhofberger
Scharzberger
Oberemmeler Rosenberg
Oberemmeler Lautersberg
Ockfener Bockstein
Ockfener Geisberg
Ockfener Herrenberg

Ayler Herrenberg
Ayler Kupp
Saarburger Rausch
Saarburger Leyenkaul
Saarburger Schlossberg
Serriger Vogelsang
Serriger Geisberg
Serriger Herrenberg

RUWER

Eitelsbacher
   Karthäuserhofberg
Eitelsbacher Wäldchen
Eitelsbacher Marienholz
Maximin-Grünhäuser
   Herrenberg

Avelsbacher Kupp
Avelsbacher Herrenberg
Caseler Taubenberg
Caseler Herrenberg
Caseler Nieschen

FRANCONIA (STEINWEIN)

Würzburger Innere Leiste
Würzburger Stein
Würzburger Leisten
Würzburger Schalksberg
Würzburger Schlossberg
Randersackerer Marsburg

Randersackerer
   Teufelskeller
Randersackerer Pfülben
Escherndorfer Lump
Escherndorfer Fürstenberg
Escherndorfer Berg

CHAPTER FIVE

THE WINES OF ITALY

Wine refreshes the stomach, sharpens the appetite, blunts care and sadness, and conduces to slumber.   —PLINY

Since the days, long before the beginning of the Christian Era, when the Greeks called the Italians *Œnotrii viri* (men of Wineland), Italy has been a great wine-producing country, and statistics show that one seventh of her entire agricultural area is planted with the vine.

With soil, climate, and all natural conditions in her favor, Italy, up to fairly recent times, has run to quantity rather than to elegance in wine. It is a matter of national attitude. The Italian is casual and easy-going about wine. Almost every farmer makes his own wine, and often his rows of vines are interspersed with vegetables. Wine-growing in other countries has been a well-ordered business, but, with certain exceptions, the Italians have for ages made their wine with a dashing sort of carelessness. Little attention has been paid to the fine points of wine-growing, as for instance, the suitability of certain

vines to certain soil and exposure. Vines were allowed
to grow much as they happened to grow; when
clipped they were attacked without benefit of sci-
ence; in the wine-making season the day's harvest
was often dumped into a vat with the previous days'
sour residue and allowed to ferment with old skins,
stems, and pips; and little wine was permitted to age.
All such wearisome details had little appeal for the
Italian. He drank—and still drinks—his wine with
the same gusto he puts into singing an aria from
Leoncavallo or Puccini. When made with a measure
of care, his red wine, which is usually better than his
white, comes out dark, robust, and fruity, and there's
no doubt that the Italian peasants who drink their
own casual brews come off rather better than the
French peasants who drink the thin, "puckery" wine
that is the *ordinaire* of many parts of France.

The Italian wine laws, which came into force about
1930, sought to bring the industry into some sem-
blance of line, and they are splendid. Indeed they
are so far superior to the earlier laws of France and
other countries that one can hope the Fascist government had time to step out from behind the bars and
take a final bow before the current was switched
on. This is not to say that attempts were made to
regulate all wine-making in Italy. Much of it has
continued in its old amateur fashion. But it does
mean that the best wine and the best-known, the
wines generally sent out for export, have been
standardized so that the buyer can put trust in the

genuineness of the product. To deserve the name it carries on its label a wine must have been grown from a specified grape in a delimited area and made by proper methods. When the wine has passed all tests, chemical and otherwise, the bottle is stamped with the "National Mark," a red-brown seal attesting to its honesty.

The laws corrected many ancient evils, one of the most annoying and confusing being a slackness about authenticity of origin. In the old days wines were named for the grapes from which they were made rather than for the region of origin. In various parts of Italy one would encounter identical names applied to wines having only the remotest family resemblance. And when place names were given to wines, one might find that the wines so named were but little grown in the regions mentioned on their labels, but were produced anywhere and everywhere. After the passage of the laws one could for the first time be sure that wine labeled "Chianti" had been grown in the officially delimited Chianti area in Tuscany, that wine labeled "Vesuvio" was grown on the Vesuvian slope, and that wine called "Capri," beloved by Tiberius and James Montgomery Flagg, came from Capri and not from Ischia. Wines of similar type, which formerly used these and other place names without the right to them, must now be marked as *Tipo* Chianti, *Tipo* Capri, etc.

The practice under which each small grower made his own wine has been gradually replaced by a *cantina* system, whereunder the grapes of all the growers of a given district go into the same press, making an average regional product. This arrangement, while it reacts unfavorably upon a few growers who had usually made good wines, has the benefit of raising general quality and of being economical as well as of insuring honesty of designation.

In 1953 the wine laws were augmented to include provisions governing wines made for export, and covering the making of Vermouth and other *apéritifs*.

Many of the wines seen before the war carried vintage years. This is something new. Formerly it was not the custom of Italians to pay any great attention to vintage years. If you lived in Italy you knew about good years and bad years simply because people talked about them. But the talk was only of the current year. If it was a good year, the word would get about, and discerning folk would go off into the country, taste wines, and select a barrel or two which later they would bottle at home. It was a pleasant custom.

Francis Brett Young, the British novelist, had a house in Capri; he and the late Edwin Cerio, author of *Aria da Capri,* always knew where the best Gragnano was to be had. In a good year they would buy a cask between them and bottle it in Cerio's living-room, which, as the bottling party proceeded, gradually assumed the appearance of a shambles, floor, walls, and workers being covered with the rich red blood of the grape. Their best Gragnano would not be more than two or three years old, and it had the qualities of a strong and noble wine—a wine that in France would have been left for three years or more in the cask, to mature, and after that would lie years longer in the bottle, ruminating and improving.

I have a strong suspicion that aging beyond a certain point does not do much for Italian wines. They are big and gusty when young, very full and rather rough, and I suspect that they are then at their best. Some years ago an Italian friend, Enrico Serafino, of Canale, sent me several bottles of very old wines—wines of 1908. One, a Barolo, opened in 1937, was a coarse wine even at its age. After opening, it needed two hours of airing to bring it to its best, and then, while undeniably a good wine, it was lacking in mellowness and finish. The second bottle, opened in 1939, was a lovely wine, the finest Italian wine I ever tasted, but it was not in a class with the great wines of the other wine-growing regions. It was a Nebbiolo Spumante, deep rose in color, like pigeon-blood ruby, with a superb bouquet. It was slightly sweet, having about the same degree of sweetness as an Anjou, Château de Bellevue, and was no longer sparkling. Both bottles discharged heavy coagulated red dregs, which is not surprising as wine in the olden days was bottled with some of the solid parts of the grape.

Italy at one time was the largest producer of wine in Europe. How it rates now is difficult to say, but certainly one can say that no other country produces such a variety of types of wine. The best are the reds; the whites tend to be either astringent or too sweet. Many are naturally sparkling. This is due to their having been bottled young, off the "short" lees, and continuing to ferment in bottle. There are a number of "manufactured" sparkling wines, the best known being Asti Spumante, a sweet wine made from the Moscato grape. Other and better sparkling wines are made by the champagne process using the Pinot grape, and these are relatively dry. The wines of northern Italy are as a rule heavier than Tuscan and southern wines. The most delicate Italian wines are some of the reds: Chianti, Brachetto, Capri, etc., which are good table wines for general service. Among the best of the heavy red wines are Barolo, Freisa, Nebbiolo, Valpolicella, Gragnano, and Barbera. Leading white wines are Soave, Frascati, Orvieto, Lacrima Christi, Capri, and Chianti Bianca. If I were to hazard a guess as to which is the best red wine made in Italy, I should say that it is probably Chianti *stravecchio*—the latter word denoting a very old wine, which in Italy means ten years or thereabouts. Of the white wines, too, I should select a good Chianti.

Italy has some famous names among her wines, none more so than Lacrima Christi. I had my first taste of it during a memorable night spent on Vesuvius during the eruption of 1906. For some weeks before the final violence in which the cone blew off we watched the angry mountain from Capri. The crater flamed like a great blast furnace, enormous clouds of smoke writhed above it, and streams of molten lava on the slope, eighteen or twenty miles away, were clearly visible. Early in April I went to the mainland with a companion and ascended the mountain at night to see the show at close range. It was a night of cold, rain, fatigue, smothering darkness, reluctant nags, and even more reluctant guides. At frequent intervals we heard subterranean boomings and saw a hot glow in the sky above the crater.

Toward three in the morning we came to a house situated higher than any other on the mountain. It was called the Casa Bianca, and the guides assured us that the family of wine-growers who lived there gladly provided hospitality at any time of day or night for a small consideration. A nerveless family they must have been, for in spite of the fact that a stream of red-hot lava was moving down the slope not far away, it took much shouting and pounding upon doors to rouse them from their slumbers.

Presently through the windows we saw them coming with candles to let us in. Smiling and chattering, they produced a noble brown loaf, a handsome cheese, and bottles of sparkling Lacrima Christi corked with mushroom-topped champagne corks tied with string.

The wine was dry and amazingly good, and when I praised it our host took up a lantern and led us out to a cave tunnelled into the mountainside where his casks and bottles of wine were stored.

"Don't you feel uneasy up here," I asked, "when the mountain is behaving so badly?"

"This volcanic soil," he answered, "is perfect for the vine, and my house is well placed. It is safe enough. My father and my grandfather lived here, and I myself have twice seen the mountain as bad as this."

A few days later the big explosion came. The cone blew off and people in villages far down the slope were killed. For a day or two I wondered anxiously about the Casa Bianca and its family. Then I found an item in the *Corriere*. The house had been buried under a stream of lava that rose at the rate of three meters a minute, but the family had escaped. Often since then I have thought of the tunnel with its wine casks far beneath that murderous crust.

Was the wine I drank that night as good as I thought it, or were palate and memory tricked by occasion and appetite? Bottles of Lacrima Christi subsequently tasted shook my faith in my first judgment. Some were still and some sparkling, but always they were sweet and unpleasant, and when in 1935 I was tasting wines for the St. Regis and a bottle turned up, I tasted it with some trepidation. And lo, there it was again, a charming wine, fragrant, golden, admirably balanced between sweet and dry, as good in 1935 as it had been in 1906.

In Sicily, as in the rest of Italy, much wine is grown in rather casual fashion for the grower's own use. Some of it is poor and some tastes pretty good, especially when it comes cool from the cask to one who has been tramping uphill under the hot sun.

Among Sicilian table wines that are commercially bottled the two most favorably known are Corvo and Zucco, both grown near Palermo. My experience has been that none but the sweet is passable. The sweet Zucco produced on the Sicilian estate of the Duke of Orleans is said to be considerably esteemed by French royalists and by the Italian colony in London.

Besides the term *stravecchio*, already mentioned, the terminology of wine in Italy includes the words *vecchio*, old; *secco*, dry; and *aboccato*, somewhat sweet.

There are many French wines that would be thought too regal to accompany anything but the choicest game or other sumptuous dishes, but among Italian wines none such exist. Italian wines are sound and vigorous but not elegant, and they are entirely at home with chicken, spaghetti, or the food one takes on a picnic. The sweet and fortified wines are, of course, excepted.

PRINCIPAL ITALIAN WINES

SOME WELL-KNOWN RED WINES

Piedmont

Barolo	Grignolino
Barbera	Freisa
Barbaresco	Gattinara
Nebbiolo	Brachetto

SOME WELL-KNOWN RED WINES—*continued*

Lombardy
Valtellina and its types:
Sassella
Inferno
Grumello
Grigioni

Tridentine Venetia
Lago di Caldaro
Lagrein Rosato
Santa Giustina
Santa Maddalena

Venetia
Valpolicella
Bardolino
Reciotto

Emelia
Lambrusco

Tuscany
Chianti
Brolio
Pomino
Rufina
Carmignano

Campania
Capri
Falerno
Vesuvio
Gragnano

SOME WELL-KNOWN WHITE WINES

Piedmont
Cortese
Gavi

Tridentine Venetia
Terlano
Riesling
Lacrimae Stae. Magdalenae

Venetia
Soave

Emelia
Albana

Umbria
Orvieto

Latium
Frascati
Castel Bracciano
Est Est Est

Campania
Capri
Lacrima Christi
Falerno
Ravello

Sicily
Corvo di Casteldaccia
Zucco
Etna

SPECIAL ITALIAN WINES

DESSERT WINES:
Moscato from the various localities
Malvasia from the island of Lipari
Aleatico

SPARKLING WINES
Asti Spumante

VERMOUTH (both red and white). Italian Vermouth is sweeter than French.

LIQUEUR:
Strega

CHAPTER SIX

THE FORTIFIED WINES

SHERRY, MALAGA, MADEIRA, PORT, AND MARSALA

SHERRY

The wine of Spain creepeth subtelly. —CHAUCER

Spain produces a variety of wines, some of them most agreeable, a few of which are dealt with in another chapter. Also she produces Sherry, perhaps the most widely known of all heavy wines, and one of the most celebrated.

Present-day Sherry, a blended and fortified wine, varying from delicate and dry to full and sweet, is made from grapes grown in the belt of white lime soil which lies near the town of Jerez de la Frontera. To this soil, to the climate of southern Spain, and to the skill of the blender, it owes its excellence. The blending is done most patiently and painstakingly, and as each blend must suit the taste of the part of the world to which the wine is to be sent, a considerable number of different types of wine are mixed to obtain the required flavor, body, and bouquet. Twelve to fourteen are not uncommon, and Carl Williams of Williams & Humbert once told me that as many as forty-four were used to make up the more complicated blends of his house.

The key to the blending of the several types of Sherry is the Solera, which represents not only the wealth of the individual house but its reason for being. It is the Solera system that makes it possible for each firm to keep its flavors uniform year after year, insuring, as it were, a flavorous trademark.

A Solera is a collection of casks, piled in three and sometimes four tiers, and each group, or Solera, contains basic wines of a definite character. Wines to make the blend are drawn from the casks on the lowest tier, which contain the oldest wine; the quantity drawn off is replaced with a younger wine from the casks on the second tier; the second in turn draws from the third, younger wine still; and into the casks at the top goes newer wine of the proper age and type. Thus the system is perpetuated, and since only a small quantity of the "mother-wine" is drawn off each time, very old Sherry is always a part, if only a minute part, of the wine contained in each bottle. This process is somewhat like that often followed with old Brandy, and it is Brandy that is used to fortify Sherries.

—153—

After-dinner Sherries are sweetened and colored to give them softness and their rich brown tones. This is done by adding one of several grape concentrates: *P. X.* made by pressing almost raisined grapes and adding Brandy to halt possible fermentation; *vino de color* made by boiling down grape juice and diluting it with old wine; *paxarete,* a blend of both.

I spoke earlier of the strange fermentation Sherry undergoes, the second fermentation which produces the *flor* or wine flower. The first fermentation is normal. When the wine has fallen clear, Brandy is added, the quantity varying according to the quality of the wine—the finer the wine, the less Brandy— and the second fermentation begins. The flowering can be heavy, and it is while living under this airtight blanket that the wine in the casks develops its own peculiarities and qualities. At the end of the second fermentation the wines are classified and given their identifying marks: *Palma* for the lightest and driest; *Raya* for the full and rich; *Palo Cortado,* between *Palma* and *Raya,* having some of the traits of both. These names are not used on labels.

A good natural *Fino,* made from *Palma* wine, is likely to be appreciated by Spaniards only; it is very light and is dry enough to curl your hair, and though to French, English, and American taste such a suggestion is unorthodox, it makes an excellent accompaniment to fish.

Sherry is a most useful wine. It is served, and properly so, at any time of the day, and it can be served right through a meal if one follows Professor Saintsbury's suggestion and brings on an Amontillado with the roast. For cooking, Sherry is invaluable. Turtle soup is only half complete without it, and it can transform a mediocre meat-stock soup into a poem. It is also used with terrapin and in preparing lobster *à la* Newberg—that old Delmonico invention originally called "Wenberg," but changed to "Newburg" when Mr. Delmonico quarreled with Mr. Wenberg. Many desserts likewise require Sherry, which, in this department, should be the sweet brown kind.

The principal designations of Sherry with which one needs to be familiar are:

FINO: The driest Sherry, mentioned above. A good *apéritif* for those who can take it.

VINO DE PASTO: Light Sherry, somewhat more mellow than Fino, for general use.

AMONTILLADO: A true wine of this type should be fairly dry, as it is blended from *Palma* wines that have been softened and enriched with age. The name gives no guarantee of dryness, however, as each Sherry house has its own blend, and Amontillados vary in color from pale to dark brown, and many are sweet. One reliable guide is color. A true Amontillado is quite light in body and is pale, somewhat darker than the Vino de Pasto, but with no hint of brown. For appetizers and with soup, also with entrées and roasts.

OLOROSO *and* AMOROSO: Soft and fruity wines, chiefly blended from the *Palo Cortado* wines, grape concentrate added.

OLD EAST INDIA *and* GOLDEN SHERRY: Chiefly blends of the full and rich *Raya* wines. For dessert.

∾ ∾

MALAGA

Malaga, the next famous wine of Spain after Sherry, is rather a Cinderella of the wine world. At one time it was known in England as "Mountain," and Dr. Johnson bought a dozen of Malaga in 1756 for twenty shillings. Talleyrand liked it, and it was found, along with rum, in Napoleon's traveling carriage at Waterloo. Why interest in this wine lapsed it would be hard to say, but certainly at the present time one seldom hears it mentioned.

For those interested in lovely Cinderellas, it is a wine fortified after fermentation, aged in cask, and blended. As with the heavier type Sherries, grape concentrate, or *vino de color,* is added to give the wine the desired color and full sweetness.

∾ ∾

MADEIRA

I drank Madeira at a great rate. . . .   —JOHN ADAMS
*(in a letter describing difficult
days of the Continental Congress)*

Of all wines, Madeiras are most intimately associated in fact and tradition with the earliest days of
the United States. Five years before the Boston Tea
Party, a Boston Madeira party signalized the bitter-
ness of the colonists against the King. And it was
of Madeira that Washington wrote, in a letter still
preserved, inviting Thomas Jefferson to dine with
him and sample a shipment newly arrived from
Funchal.

All of the great fortified wines are individualists,
but none more so than Madeira. It differs from the
others, not only in the characteristics given it by
soil, climate, and the method of its making, but in
its uniquely colorful past. The Madeiras we now
know are quiet stay-at-homes in comparison with
their earlier brethren. The wines have always been
matured by heat, which at the present time is given
them artificially in rooms where the temperature
varies from 100° to 160°. But at an earlier period
pipes of the best wines were picked up at the islands
and taken on long sea voyages, if possible to China
or India by way of the Cape of Good Hope, to be
improved by being shaken up and baked in the heat
of the tropics. Thus we hear of Madeira junketing
with the old windjammers and being loaded as bal-
last aboard the frigate *Constitution*. Madeira and the
Constitution had made acquaintance long before
their travels together, however. Three efforts were
made to launch this famous ship. At the first two,
which failed, water was used for the baptism, but at

the third effort a bottle of old Madeira was produced and the launching was successful.

Much of the Madeira lore has been lost to us, and part of its loss is due to the casual and inexplicit naming of the old-time wine in this country. It was the exception rather than the rule to find a Madeira designated as Sercial, Verdelho, Bual, or Malmsey— these being the names of the four principal grapes from which Madeira wines have long been made and blended. Generally Madeira brought here came to be known by the names of ships, merchants, prominent families, places, events (there was a Jenny Lind 1849, for instance), and sometimes only by initials. As the wine lives to considerable age, occasional bottles of these interestingly labeled wines turn up at auctions still. The oldest I ever owned was an 1838, John L. Cadwallader—No. 8 Bual. This wine was a century old when first I tasted it, and was as fine an old Madeira as I ever met. It was almost as big and fine as a new wine, yet had the mellowness and distinction of age.

A considerable ritual surrounded the drinking of Madeira in the old days, and a letter received long ago from Langdon Mitchell, son of S. Weir Mitchell, the gifted and lamented man who contributed *A Madeira Party* to American literature, explains about the different ways in which Madeira has been drunk in this country at various periods. In early times it was drunk in large quantities the way Port used to be drunk in England after a fox hunt. At a later period it was drunk after dinner but with no great ceremony and still in large quantities. Then, beginning in the early 1800's it came to be drunk after dinner in small quantities with great stress on the difference between the various wines. And still later, Madeira parties came into being. These parties began at four thirty in the afternoon and lasted two or three hours. There were usually eight men at table, and five wines were tasted and discussed. They circulated in old decanters on silver coasters and were pushed around the table clockwise. Biscuits and nuts were eaten, and after two wines had been tasted, Havana cigars were permitted. Madeira is, I believe, the only wine whose strict devotees allow this.

Madeira is the closest rival Sherry has. As has been pointed out before, both are remarkable for marrying the qualities of richness and dryness. Madeira may be drunk at tea time, as a prelude to dinner, with soup, with cheese, and with dessert. And as an eleven o'clock wine, with walnuts, it is incomparable.

Also, like Sherry, Madeira is a fortified wine and one of complicated structure. The wine is fermented, given the heat treatment mentioned earlier, the finer wines being treated longer and at lower temperatures than the lesser wines; it is then fortified, matured for a long period in cask, and blended with older wines and others that give to the wine the character of its house and whatever is demanded by the market to which it will go. Shippers maintain their own blends, and the name of a reliable shipper carries its own guarantee.

Madeira ranges in taste from the driest to the sweetest, the three principal kinds the following:

SERCIAL: A dry delicate wine to be drunk before dinner or with the soup.

BUAL *or* BOAL: A rich wine with a fine bouquet and perfect balance; good either at the beginning or the end of a meal.

MALMSEY *or* MALVASIA: A sweet dessert wine, or to serve at five o'clock with fruit cake.

In a special class from the point of view of popularity is Rainwater Madeira, a pale-colored wine, lighter in body than the others, yet rich in flavor and bouquet. A mystery surrounds the origin of this wine, which has been known in this country since 1820. Mr. Charles Bellows, wine-merchant and wine-scholar, who died in 1934 at the age of eighty-five, discusses the wine in a pamphlet he wrote on Madeira:

"I do not know if what causes Madeira to be Rain Water has ever been scientifically explained, but it is a freak condition of wine caused by lack of color in the grape, sudden change of temperature, starvation in the lees and . . . other natural causes, but is of so rare occurrence that the Rain Waters are highly prized as curiosities."

Rainwater has long since ceased to be a curiosity. Many shippers now market wine under this name, their methods of arriving at it their own secret. Of all fortified wines it seems to me the most pleasant, its sweetness and dryness being married to just the right point for popular taste.

∽ ∽

PORT

But in spite of all temptations
To belong to other nations,
He remains an Englishman!

—W. S. GILBERT
(*H.M.S. Pinafore*)

Port wine is as much an English institution as the House of Lords. Records of the shipment of wine from Portugal to England run back into the fourteenth century, but it was the Methuen Treaty of 1703, between Britain and Portugal, which entrenched Port as the English aristocrat's wine of wines. By the terms of this treaty, Port was admitted to England under a very light tax, and at the same time—to the great annoyance of the Claret-drinkers, who protested loudly—French wines were heavily taxed.

Not only do Englishmen like Port, but they control the business in Port all the way from the making of the wine to the sale of it, which, up to the time of the war, was mainly to their compatriots, who were its chief consumers. Shand compares the tradition of Port in England to that of fox-hunting. Every English family of pretensions had a cellar of Port as one of its prized possessions, and as the old cobwebbed bottles were brought up and consumed, new ones were purchased and laid down so that sons and grandsons would find full bins when their turn came.

This picture of beautiful living has not entirely faded out, but it has been greatly altered by changes resulting from the second great war. The cobwebbed bottles could not be replaced. Incomparably the finest of all Ports is the Vintage, all of which in years past went to England as a matter of course. With its market dried up, little wine of this quality was made in the war years. A medium-grade took its place, imported into England under a strict quota system which took no account of private cellars; and the wine was not worthy laying down. And there is the familiar tale of a new restlessness in living, of meals got through quickly and on with the dance.

A writer on these subjects, citing the quantities of Port consumed in England still, and consumed as well as made in Canada, the United States, and Australia, pronounces it a purely Anglo-Saxon drink. However, the Scandinavian countries have become the largest importers of the wine, with Belgium and Holland taking large shares. Vintage Port has grown in popularity in our own country, somewhat displacing Tawny Port, long the favorite.

The vines from which Port is made grow in the craggy hills of the mountainous region of north Portugal called Cimo do Douro. Rising from the river to the tops of the mountains are row upon row of narrow terraces where the vines push their roots down into a soil consisting largely of stone that has been hand-crushed into small bits. The Machine Age has not reached the Douro, and the first steps in the making of Port are closely associated with the folk of the countryside. Not only do peasants crush the stone to build the terraces, but they plant and tend the vines. Their wives, mothers, and sisters pick the grapes, whereat the men take over again. They carry the filled hampers, each weighing about a hundred and fifty pounds, to the wineries at the *quintas,* or farms, and there they tread the grapes, moving across the trough in two compact lines. And it is only after the great casks, taken down-river by Portuguese boatmen, have been delivered at the immense wine lodges owned by the firms trading in Port, that the countrymen's job is finished. From that point experts carry on, and the highly technical processes of selection, blending, and aging begin.

In its natural state Port is a light red wine. Various grapes possessing different qualities—some for flavor and some for color—are pressed together. The skins that give color are left in the fermenting juice until the grower determines by analysis that enough of the natural grape sugar has been transformed into alcohol, generally the third or fourth day; whereupon he doses the mass with Brandy, which abruptly stops fermentation. This leaves a certain percentage of grape sugar unfermented, to enrich the wine. It is the addition of Brandy which requires that the dark red Port made for the British market be aged for many years, to let the excess of alcohol work off. There is a long period when the Port can't quite make up its mind whether it is Brandy and wine, or wine and Brandy, but at last the Brandy weakens and the blend becomes a smooth old wine, which respectable dowagers can drink. Port should age twelve to fifteen years, and twenty-five-year-old Port is much to be preferred.

Perhaps no wine in the world receives the same degree of protection as that given to Port. Under the treaty existing between Portugal and Great Britain, Port is defined as a fortified wine produced in a strictly delimited area in the Douro region and exported through Oporto. No wine of similar character produced elsewhere is eligible to the British market, not even with a qualifying designation such as Tarragona Port. In addition, the Portuguese government protects the sale of the wine through an agency called the *Instituto do Vinho do Porto*, which not only samples the wine from each *quinta* when it arrives down-river, but checks on all wines ready for shipment. Its word is law, and the approval of the Institute must be obtained before a wine may be shipped.

The principal types of Port are these:

VINTAGE PORT: Wine of any one year, bottled about two years after being made and aged in the bottle. Vintage Port is produced only in exceptional years, and should not be drunk until it is at least twenty years old.

TAWNY PORT: Port that has been blended carefully and fully aged in the cask. It does not improve in bottle. It is lighter in strength and color than the Vintage Port. An excellent wine, more popular in the United States than red Port.

RUBY PORT: A blend of young wines with some old added. Aged in cask, can improve in bottle.

WHITE PORT: "White" in the sense that yellow wine is "white." Not cared for in England, but successful in other countries.

INVALID PORT: A Port of medium body.

MARSALA

Nunc vino pellite curas. —HORACE

Marsala is another Cinderella among fortified wines. The wine at one time was in fair demand, but now is being so far neglected that those of us who make zabaglione remember at the last moment that it is Marsala we want, and having none, we use Madeira.

Marsala is a Sicilian wine made in the city of that name from two varieties of grapes grown in the hinterland. Against the long background of Sicilian history the wine of Marsala seems quite new. It was invented in the late eighteenth century by an Englishman who frankly hoped to make it a sort of low-priced competitor to Sherry, then, as now, popular in England.

The wine is fortified with Brandy at the end of the fermentation, a boiled-down grape juice is added to give it sweetness and color, it is matured in cask and blended. Some of the export markings for Marsala are: L.P., London Particular; O.P., Old Particular; S.O.M., Superior Old Marsala. Good Marsala made by the Florio firm with a generous blending of old wine can be an excellent wine in its own right. I remember having an Old Particular in London many years ago which seemed to me not too unlike a good old Madeira. Marsala is a necessary ingredient in many Italian desserts, and the dry makes a pleasant *apéritif*.

In 1800, when Lord Nelson, who owned the Sicilian title Duke of Bronté, was on guard in the Mediterranean against Napoleon, he purchased for his fleet, as a specific against scurvy, five hundred pipes of Marsala, which he praised to the skies.

CHAPTER SEVEN

OTHER ANCIENT WINE LANDS

THE WINES OF
HUNGARY, SWITZERLAND,
SPAIN, PORTUGAL, PALESTINE,
PERSIA, GREECE,
AND RUSSIA

One of the most commendable things about wine is its limitless and fascinating variety, not only within each country, but throughout the world. Wine is made wherever grapes will grow, and I have found endless enjoyment in collecting and sampling as many of the world's vinicultural products as I could reach. The most satisfactory way to taste a representative lot is to visit the country where each is made, since some of the wines are not exported, as for instance, the Russian, and some are made in such small quantity the entire output is consumed on the spot. But wines from all of the big- and many of the small-producing countries do come to us, and the best advice I can give the jaded or aspiring wine-lover is to play the field. In this pursuit there is little danger of boredom or monotony. Tracking down odd and unfamiliar bottles is an absorbing business, and the moment of waiting for the wine to reveal itself can be exciting.

∽ ∽

HUNGARY

Up jumped Tokay on our table,
Like a pygmy castle-warder,
Dwarfish to see, but stout and able,
Arms and accoutrements all in order. . . .
—ROBERT BROWNING

Hungary is one of the principal wine-producing countries of the world, and this fact has been too little recognized. When Arpad and his hordes came trailing into Hungary in the ninth century, they found there vines that had been planted by the Romans. Many wines are made in Hungary, almost every province contributing one or more of excellent quality. As happens so often, however, the many good are overshadowed by the one great, in this case the famous Tokay, which at its peak has every right to its fame.

The lesser-known wines of Hungary are found in an exceptional range of flavors and kinds, as I learned in 1928 when I spent a month there, tasting Hungarian wines. There was a sturdy, full red wine called Egri Bikavér, or "Bull's Blood of Eger"; several called Rizling, and a Badacsonyi Rizling, which were very nice wines, rather suggesting good German wines but with characteristic distinctly their own; a Smolyói Furmint, whose bouquet was like none other I ever met. Another wine of the Badacsonyi region, which is near Lake Balaton, Szürkebarát, was a nice grapy wine with a pleasant bouquet, and Szilváni, greenish in color, was very smooth with a honeylike overtone.

But the big show is and always has been Tokay. There are three top grades of this wine, the result of different methods of making, and the finest of them, and one of the magnificent wines of the world, is the Essence. Tokay Essence, which is valued highly as a tonic for the sick and is very costly, has been described as an attar of grapes. It is made only in great years. The grapes, ripened as for the great Yquems and the Trockenbeeren Ausleses, are gathered late and piled in a vat, and the Essence is made from the juice that comes from them naturally, under the pressure of their own weight. This special juice constitutes only about one two-hundred-and-fiftieth part of the total amount yielded by the grapes later, under pressure. Rich in sugar, the Essence ferments very slowly and forms but little alcohol. It is said not to improve after about fifty years, but to have a life that is practically limitless.

In one of the cellar-books appears a label of a

Tokay Essence of 1811, a wine said by a friend who still has a few bottles in his cellar to be perfection, showing not the least sign of imminent decline. Wines of such rarity often have a story to tell, and the 1811 is no exception. Berry Brothers of London, and particularly Mr. Charles Berry, who sent the wine, are unique among the wine-merchants of the world. Not only do the members of the firm sell wine, but they know it, enjoy it, write books about it, and more important, they are constantly turning up treasures, wines sometimes brought from secret hiding places, and not infrequently, long forgotten. The Cachet de Liége, mentioned earlier, was one of their discoveries. When choice wine comes into his hands, it is Mr. Berry's custom to garb it beautifully, designing a label worthy of it, and one of the most attractive examples of Mr. Berry's dreaming adorns the Essence of 1811. Surmounted by an imposing and colorful coat-of-arms, the label states that the wine was grown and bottled on the property of the Princely Family of Britzenheim, which became extinct in 1863. The wine was walled-in during the Hungarian Revolution of 1849, and was rediscovered in 1925 when it was imported into England by Berry Brothers.

One fact Mr. Berry neglected to mention: 1811 was the Year of the Comet, a year so great in wines that they were still being discussed in awed tones more than a hundred years later. However, the year is not alone responsible for the long and healthy life of this particular wine. Its age is not uncommon. There is, for example, the newspaper account of the marriage of the President of Poland, in 1933, which contained the information that the health of the bride and bridegroom was drunk in wine two hundred and fifty years old. The wine, if good, could only have been Essence of Tokay, and the centuries-old traditional friendship between Poland and Hungary would seem to support this conclusion.

The Aszu, also called Ausbruch, is only a little less fine than the Essence, and is rated one of the three greatest natural dessert wines of the world, the other two being Yquem and the Trockenbeeren Ausleses of Germany. The Aszu is made by crushing the shriveled and "nobly-molded" grapes used to make the Essence, or others equally raisined, and adding the crush to the fermenting juice of normally ripened berries. The addition is made by strict measure, in this case a *puttony*, which is approximately seven and a half gallons. Depending upon the number of *puttonyos* of the dried Aszu grapes that are added to a cask containing thirty-five gallons of the ordinary dry wine, the finished product is classified as 2, 3, 5, and occasionally 9 *puttonyos*, and the number is indicated on the label of each bottle, the higher the number, the richer the wine.

The third variety, Szamorodni, also a fine wine, is the driest of the group unless made in a hot year, when the fact of its sweetness is indicated on the label.

While staying in Hungary I sought to find a great Tokay or Tokay Essence, but I found none of the latter, and though I tasted good Tokays of both the Szamorodni and Aszu varieties, I never found one to compare with a Tokay I had tasted at home the year before.

Ten or a dozen years earlier a friend of mine had been dangerously ill and I wished to take him some very fine old Port. I went to Mr. Niles, manager of Delmonico's, explained my need, and was told that some Charleston Jockey Club Port of 1842 was the best in his cellars.

"But I have something very much finer than that," he said, and he showed me an astonishing bottle of Tokay. There was no date upon the bottle, but it was obviously very, very old, a hand-made bottle of odd shape, green and picturesque, with a seal stamped in the glass, a faded label written by hand in an old-time foreign script, and the Spanish War tax stamp the newest thing in sight.

I took it to my friend at the hospital and he asked me to place it on the mantelpiece where he could see it from his bed.

"The doctors wouldn't let me drink it," he told me a month or two later, when he had recovered, "but we'll have it after a while when they let up on me."

In the next year or two he spoke to me several times of the Tokay. Still the doctors would not let him have it, but some day he would open it, and I should be there when he did.

The first World War came, and after a while we were drawn in. A soldier and a natural leader, my friend wished to raise a division and lead it to France, but President Wilson would not permit him to. His four sons went, however, and life was very trying for him, but still he would speak now and then about the wine.

"We'll drink it when the boys come home," he said.

But not all the boys did come home. One was buried by the Germans where he fell when his airplane was shot down, and the others were still in uniform, still abroad, when, two months after the signing of the Armistice, their father died.

I had forgotten the Tokay, but one day during the summer following his death a package was delivered at my house. It was from his widow, and it contained the ancient bottle I had given him years before.

It became, naturally, one of my foremost treasures, and I used to wonder sometimes whether I should ever meet with an occasion great enough to justify its being opened.

In 1927 the occasion came. The fragrance of grapes gathered well over a hundred years before in the Carpathian foothills was released in a diningroom at Princeton, New Jersey, and the health of a young couple dear to my heart was drunk in what, to me and mine, had long since ceased to figure by its actual name, Imperial Aszu, and had become the "Roosevelt Tokay."

〜 〜

SWITZERLAND

To happy convents, bosom'd deep in vines,
Where slumber abbots purple as their wines.
—ALEXANDER POPE

The history of viticulture in Switzerland is similar to that of France and Germany. The vineyards were planted by the Romans and later taken over by the monasteries; growth and progress were checked by the phylloxera, and when wine-growing was resumed, it was slightly altered and on a smaller scale. As everywhere in Europe, the monks were splendid wine-makers, and production under their hands grew to the point where the vine threatened to engulf the small nation, and its planting had finally to be restricted by edict. At the present time Switzerland has about 33,500 acres in vines and a yield that varies greatly in good and bad years but is approximately 2,900,000 gallons of red wine and 11,600,000 gallons of white. Production is not large enough to permit of much exportation—the Swiss like their own wines. All wine-lists of any consequence, however, now carry a small number of Swiss wines.

The best of the wines are white, and faintly sug-

gest those of Alsace and the lighter wines of the
Rhine; the red wines, although made of the black
Pinot, have little resemblance to Burgundy, lacking
its mellow qualities and tending to be almost too
full-bodied.

In the main, Swiss wines should be drunk young,
and actually that urgency is inherent in the wines
themselves. They have a freshness that demands enjoyment before it fades. A number of the wines will
be found to have a small but perceptible sparkle,
rather like certain of the Moselles. They are bottled
off the short lees, after the first racking, and a part
of the natural fermentation is thus caught and held.

The principal wine-making districts are the can-
tons of Vaud, Valais, and Neuchâtel. Each produces
many "small" regional wines and a limited number
of wines of better quality. Of the latter, some are
too delicate to travel but others have found their way
to our market.

The best known growth of Vaud is Dézaley, or
Dézaley de la Ville de Lausanne, a group of vineyards owned by the city of Lausanne. The wines are
sold at auction, then bottled under the eye of the
city, provided with an official label and cork, and
sold as Dézaley or with a vineyard name attached,
such as Clos des Abbeyes and Clos des Moines.
Other well-known properties in the Dézaley region
are Clos de la Borne and Les Embleyres.

Vaudois wines are made also in La Côte where
especially fine dry white wines are grown at old es-

tates with picturesque names: Château de Luins, Mont sur Rolle, and the Abbey de Mont.

The canton of Valais, which includes the region of the upper Rhône Valley, is perhaps the most important of the wine districts. The vineyards are protected on the north and south by the accommodating Alps, and the climate during the growing season is dry and hot. The best-known wines from this region are Fendant Molignon, Johannisberg, made of the Riesling grape, and Clos de Montibeaux, Fendant St.-Michel, Brule Fer, and Domaine de Mont d'Or. Also made in Valais is the very interesting Vin du Glacier, a wine aged for several years in wood and kept at a high altitude.

At the foot of the Jura Mountains grows the chummy little wine Neuchâtel. This wine is seldom sold under any but its simple designation. It can be a delightful wine, light-bodied, with a nice individual freshness.

∽ ∾

SPAIN

I have trodden the winepress alone. . . .
—ISAIAH LXIII, 3

Spain and Portugal make a number of very acceptable natural table wines, which again are overshadowed by the more celebrated product of each country, Sherry and Port.

Grapes have grown in almost every part of Spain since time immemorial, and its red and white wines have been recognized exports since the Roman era. However, the first bottles shipped into this country on the resumption of legal imports contained coarse wines, unquestionably second-rate, and the unfortunate reputation thus created disappeared only with improved quality. The Spanish wines we now receive are deserving of attention.

The best table wines are made in the northern part of the country, in the valley of the Ebro, in Catalonia, in certain regions along the Mediterranean Coast, and in a small district surrounding the town of Valdepeñas. In the Ebro Valley, from whence come the Riojas, French methods of wine-making are followed, an inheritance from the wine-growers who transferred their efforts to Spain when the French vineyards were destroyed by the phylloxera. The settlers departed in time to replant their own vineyards, but the knowledge of wine-making they had brought with them remained behind in Spain.

The Riojas, red and white, are considered the finest of the table wines. Although modest and making no pretense of greatness, and in essence typical of their rigorous land, they have something of the dimensions of French wines of comparable class, and are reliable and good. There are a number of competent firms in this district, among them Bodegas Bilbainas, the

Marqués de Riscal, the Marqués de Murrieta, and Bodegas Francos-Españoles.

From the province of Catalonia come a number of good wines, the red and white Castell Del Remy and the Alella wines. The white wines of this district are better than the reds as a rule. An Alella Legitimo made by the Bodega Alella Vinicola proved to be a pale, light-bodied wine, a little on the sweet side, an admirable wine for summer lunches on the terrace. And the wines of Valdepeñas, red and white, are big wines, sturdy and well balanced, and of better than average quality.

~ ~

PORTUGAL

During the Peninsular War, Wellington acquired a taste for Carcavelos Wine, as did many of his officers, and they took this liking back to England with them.

—Portuguese Government Bulletin

The Portuguese are proud of the place their country has occupied in the long vinicultural history of Europe, and they consider that both the rich wine lore and the pleasant product of today are receiving far too little attention.

Portuguese table wines come in a considerable variety, actually, and my impression is that the white wines are better than the reds. The red wines seem either too heavily tannined, or to have the sharp unnatural taste one rightly or wrongly associates with artificial treatment or with wines made from grapes picked before they were ripe. The best of the reds of Collares can be expected.

As to the white wines, most of those tasted seemed to be low in acidity and to have a variable degree of sweetness. When the wines are frankly sweet they are better than average. Ferra Quente has the qualities of a Second *Cru* Sauternes, and Chello suggests a five-o'clock snack, with dry biscuits and *foie gras*. Chello is sold in a blue-and-white pottery bottle, and since every woman seeing it will yearn to transform the bottle into a lamp, or use it as a vase, its packaging should contribute greatly to the sale of the wine. A Mateusa, contained in a squat Steinwein bottle, was honest and unpretentious, and there is another nice Mateusa, a *vin rosé;* and also a very pleasant light wine called Camarate. The best-known of Portuguese table wines, undoubtedly, is Lancers Crackling Rosé, which is pink, sparkling, and middling sweet. Almost surely, in an earlier time, this *rosé* would have been called "ladies' wine." It is another for the odd hour, best served with simple wafers containing little sugar.

A type of wine much liked by the Portuguese but having a mixed appeal for outsiders is the famous "Green" wine, *Vinho Verde,* both red and white. The "Greens" are immature wines, sometimes sparkling and heady, which are said by their devotees to be comforting and refreshing on a hot day. It is still the custom in Portugal, and a very nice custom it is, to serve open wine with meals in restaurants, including it in the over-all price. More often than not, the carafes contain a "Green" wine.

❦ ❦

PALESTINE

Therefore God give thee of the dew of heaven, and the fatness of the earth, and plenty of corn and wine.
—Genesis xxvii: 28

An impressive amount of wine is being made in Palestine, the era of small scattered vineyards and the general drought of Arab and Moslem rule having ended some fifty or more years ago. Those I tasted were heavy and sweet, called Port and Sherry, but having little likeness to the parent wines. A certain degree of sweetness is inevitable in Palestinian wines —at least, in those made from fully ripened grapes— because of the heat and aridity of the region where they are grown.

❦ ❦

PERSIA

There is great reason to believe that, among the many benefits that Persia has conferred upon mankind, we owe to her the delightful gift of wine.   —Sir Percy Sykes

Another Moslem country where wine is made on a limited scale is Persia. The best comes from Shiraz, where the vines are grown in unirrigated vineyards planted on the barren sides of mountains. Since the true Moslem must not drink wine, it is made, and presumably consumed, by the Parsis and the Armenians. Persia, by the way, lays claim to the first record of bootlegging. To quote from Janet Miller's *Camel-Bells of Bagdad:*[1] "After the Moslem Conquest . . . the upper classes continued to drink in secret. The poet Hafiz (who died about 1390) writes:

> 'Bring wine. Let first the hand of Hafiz
> The cheering cup embrace,
> Yet only on one condition—
> No word beyond this place.' "

∽ ∽

GREECE

Bronze is the mirror of the form; wine of the heart.

—AESCHYLUS

One can occasionally find Greek wines in the market. In the ancient days of wine-making on the peninsula, resin was used as a preservative, a piece being put into each barrel; and while its use still continues, tending to cut the popularity of this Greek product, unresinated wines have become more in demand and it is from these that selection is made for export. I have thus far found no trace of resin in the Greek wines I have tasted. These included a Beso Roditys, a light, red table wine that was exceedingly agreeable, certainly better than many Italian wines

[1] Houghton Mifflin Company, 1934.

of reputation; Mavrodaphne, a dessert wine of the heavy Port-Sherry-Madeira type, sweet, clean, and quite interesting; and Barbaresso "Dionysos" Brandy, which turned out to be a nice smooth Brandy with no suggestion of unpleasant flavor.

∽ ∽

RUSSIA

Comrade, have you ever drained a water glass filled with Russian rum or vodka?   —KENNETH L. DIXON

It is odd that among reports sent back by travelers to Russia there is little mention of Russian wines. As with everything Russian, wine assumes increasing importance if for no other reason than their declaration that by 1970 they will be outproducing France in quality as well as in quantity. With half the northern earth to plant over, quantity should be no problem; quality is another matter. Quality in France is not alone the consequence of sun, soil, and vinification know-how; it is primarily an expression of the sophisticated taste of a people, the mark of a race.

And Russian taste? Most impressive is their robust and impulsive vitality, which seems to take little account of refinement or sophistication, and perhaps the living thing that is wine will be found to exhibit, in some measure at least, the wide divergence in national character.

The *Memoirs of the Comte de Rochechourart* tell

us that the Empress Catherine II gave a large estate in the Crimea to Prince Potemkin, who planted the whole valley of Soudak with vines brought from Bordeaux, Burgundy, Spain, and Madeira. He built enormous cellars and, from all reports, made some quite good wine. The Soviet Government absorbed what remained of this and neighboring enterprises, expanded the plantings, and the Crimea continues to produce the best of the sweet and dessert wines, one of the latter resembling Malmsey Madeira, and others Port, Sherry, and Tokay. Full-bodied dessert wines are made also in Uzbekistan, Armenia, and Azerbaijan, where the Muscat grape is extensively grown.

Wines well remembered from past years are made in the Ukraine, in a section of Bessarabia which belonged formerly to Rumania. The vines are of prime stock and the wine history is a fairly long one. Table wines are made also in sections of Georgia, and in the North and South Caucasus.

Champagne comes chiefly from the North Caucasus, where the soil and climate combine to ensure the correct sugar-acid ratio required for the making of the finest varieties of this wine. Other Champagne districts are found in Transcaucasia, Don, and Kazakhstan; and wine grapes have been planted in Uzbekistan, which in former years, with Kazakhstan, was known for the excellence of table varieties.

Brandy, in grades distinguished by the well-known stars, is made in Armenia, Georgia, and Azerbaijan. In opposition to the French practice, which is to make their Cognacs by distilling wines not pleasant to drink, the Russians use high-class table wines.

In the absence of wines to taste, one must conjecture about the characteristics of the wines from knowledge of the grapes which make them: Pinot, Traminer, Aligote, Semillon, Sylvaner, Riesling, Cabernet Sauvignon, and others, all imported from the West. Their *Riesling Abrau* and *Silvaner,* both natives of Georgia, could be very nice wines. In the listing of grape varieties, "and local sorts" is included, suggesting that they make use of native vines when these are found.

Wine is a farm product, made in Russia on the collectives. In discussing this subject, a wine-wise friend remarked: "Good wine comes from God, working through a combination of vines, soil, and man." The question is how well the combination is permitted to work in Russia. The making of wine, fine or even good, requires not only the special skills of a farmer but a kind of inspired artistry, and not until the wines are here in easily available quantities will we know how sympathetic the Soviet system is to this need for creative freedom.

My favorite story about Russian wine involves two American girls who wandered for some months in Russia in 1927 and 1928 with, as one phrased it, nothing more lethal in the way of a protective weapon than a nail scissors. They were much taken with a wine whose Russian characters spelled phonetically *Shah-Toe-Ee-Kem.*

CHAPTER EIGHT

THE WINES OF THE
UNITED STATES

Alcohol is habit-forming, just like olives. You know how
that works. When I was a young girl and olives came to
this country, I couldn't eat one. I choked and gagged
when they gave them to me at parties. Then, one day, I
was restless. I wanted to eat something, but I didn't know
what it was. Then suddenly I knew it was an olive. I ate
one and I knew I had the habit.

—MRS. IDA B. WISE SMITH
President of the W.C.T.U.
(Interview in the *New York Sun*,
November 23, 1933)

An impressive total of 156,203,000 gallons of wine
was consumed in this country last year, eighty per
cent made in California, something more than fourteen per cent in the Eastern states, and the remainder
imported from Europe. The figure is not quite so impressive when it is broken down into its component
parts, and the facts on domestic production reveal
that table wines accounted for only slightly more
than one quarter of the total, the remainder sweet

and dessert types and the great quantity of *vin ordinaire* that is shipped by sea in tankers and over-land in tank cars, and rests in gallon jugs on the lower shelves of wine-shops. The last-named appears in varieties of both red and white, and is completely standardized, individual items in either category often indistinguishable the one from the other. Selection from among them is no problem.

CALIFORNIA

Philip M. Wagner states in *A Wine-Grower's Guide*[1]: ". . . the key to quality lies in the character of the grapes from which wine is made."

Even though choice vines from Europe have been planted in California for a hundred and fifty years or more, it took rather a long time for this statement to be generally appreciated by present-day growers. A few of the more aspiring or idealistic made great efforts to fill their vineyards with guaranteed wine-grape stock, but immediately after Repeal and for a number of years thereafter, continuing to some extent into the present, wine was made from inferior grapes, or from grapes not intended for wine-making at all. Part of this has been done knowingly, but part has resulted from honest confusion as to the identity of the vines planted. All too frequently when cuttings of top quality were sought abroad, misnamed cuttings of inferior varieties were purposely substituted

[1] New York: Alfred A. Knopf; 1956.

for those ordered. This fraudulent traffic in vine cuttings, mentioned in the earliest vineyard records, continued into the 1930's and it wasn't until the University of California's Division of Viticulture undertook to unravel the snarl that a grower was entirely certain which varieties were making his wines.

The move into varietal plantings has been steady in the last dozen years; what point it has reached is a question only the flavor of the wines can answer. The grapes which make the bulk of the wines of the world, both great and small, are varieties of the species *Vitis vinifera*. Understandably, the flavor of the individual grape is altered somewhat by differences in soil and climate, but if the wine resulting is well and honestly made, it must retain something of the accepted character of the original growth. Thus, if one buys a California wine labeled Cabernet Sauvignon, one may expect to find the family flavor of the Bordeaux wines made in France.

Considering the pre-eminent growths, Cabernet Sauvignon seems to find the soil and climate of California much more congenial than Pinot noir. The latter is a cranky grape whose yield is small, which requires an individual pruning system, careful determination as to the exact time for the crushing of the grapes, and special storage conditions for the maturing wine. Plantings of it are still not numerous. In a tasting of a group of California Pinot noirs the wines seemed to have scant parental resemblance. Martin Ray's Pinot Noir is excepted. In comparative tastings of groups of the two finest of the white grapes, the Rieslings and Chardonnays fared somewhat better.

It has been said that these highly bred varieties don't give of their best in California, the sun and heat combining to enrich the grapes at the expense of acid. The northern coastal sections, and particularly the vineyards placed at some altitude in the hills, are recommended for the growing of the prime varieties. Cool weather, even a touch of real cold, and light breezes retard the growth in the vines, develop more acid and reduce the sugar content of the grapes; and from the vineyards so placed come the best of California's table and sparkling wines.

The Sauternes grapes, Semillon and Sauvignon blanc, produce only an occasional wine which recalls the French original. However, they grow without too great coddling and the wines they make are, in the main, dry. Their names are spelled variously: Sauternes, Sauterne, Sautern.

California wines have ever presented a confused face to the earnest seeker after the best of them. In former days growers anxious for an opinion shipped cases of their wines to this household, and many of them were extremely good. Often they were served to guests who, in appreciation of them, jotted down the names and other information. It became almost the rule to expect to hear, on next meeting, such deflated comment as: "You remember the wine you gave us last week? I bought a case. The bottle *looks* all right—the label is identical with yours, but the wine is not the same." And there are the state fairs and their much advertised prizes. A short while ago, at a tasting of California white wines, one of the guests was heard to mutter: "You won no prize, my lad." And yet boastfully displayed on the label of the bottle was the legend of a first prize given over many years. Obviously, not the same wine.

California can make very fine wines, does make such; but with the exception of a few superior brands pridefully marketed by their growers, wine of the exhibition class seldom reaches the market.

How then can one go about making selection from among these wines? Principally by searching out the best of the varietal wines made by the most responsible houses. According to federal law, a varietal wine, so named for one grape, must contain not less than 51 per cent of wine made from the grape whose name it bears; which means that there *should* be a sufficient quantity of the paramount grape to guide one in choosing wisely once the distinguishing flavor of the grape is known. The best of the varietals will have on the label the full name of the grape, and be made in the region best suited to the growing of that grape.

Varietal wines made from secondary grapes sometimes have a misleading sound of importance: Black Pinot, White Pinot, Pinot St. George, Sauvignon Vert, to name a few. They have no kinship to the great ones, and should be bought on their own attractions and not because of a looked-for similarity to their peers.

Next in order, the types named for European wine-making regions: Burgundy, Claret or Bordeaux, Rhine, Chablis, etc. They are blended wines, and since few firms grow all the grapes required for the making of the extensive lists shipped under their names, the wines are blended from a number of kinds of grapes to a quality the firms set as standard. The question always presents itself: why bother with these when other types are being made so much more successfully? They are cheap, of course, which isn't synonymous with a good buy. The reds often seem interchangeable, and the whites too heavily sulphured.

California is a large producer of Champagne, including the pink and the red. The best of it is made by the time-honored bottle-fermented process introduced from France, the lesser quality by the vat method called *Charmat*, also derived from the French, and a third by carbonation. The label takes account of each type. Occasionally one hears the criticism that California Champagnes have a flat taste. The acid content of this wine is of the greatest importance. It can happen in Reims and Epernay that the picking of the grapes is delayed too long, each day in the sun increasing the sugar and decreasing the acid, and when that occurs the growers hasten about their job with anxious faces. Their California confreres have that problem perpetually, so it follows that the best Champagnes come from the coolest of the growing regions, from vineyards with plantings of the Pinot noir and Chardonnay, the grapes which make the fine originals. The descriptive designations of California Champagnes, from *brut* to *doux*, correspond to those laid down in France.

Most of the vineyards now concern themselves with *rosé* wines. The Grenache grape makes the best of these, and admirers of *rosé* wines consider them first-rate of their kind, although it must be noted that variety ranges rather widely, depending upon the maker. In a rare class by itself is Pinot Noir Rosé made by Martin Ray.

California Sherries seem not to have too much to recommend them, but some of the Ports are good. The Sherries should be considered purely from one's taste in fortified or *apéritif* wines, as there is little resemblance between them and the true Spanish types. One which made its bow with great fanfare several years ago tasted like an amateur's attempt at Vermouth. The brilliant œnological group at the University of California's Division of Viticulture located at Davis, whose best-known member is Dr. Maynard Amerine, has completed studies of the second fermentation of Spanish Sherries, that mysterious development which occurs under a tight blanket of the wine's own *flor*. Gradually this method is replacing those formerly in use.

One hears increasingly of the excellence of the Ports made by Ficklin Vineyards, at Madera in

Fresno County. Limiting themselves to the production of the one wine, the Ficklin family has planted the finest of the Portuguese grape varieties and is making its wines with care and skill. They are recommended to the attention of the lovers of Port.

As to Brandies, the Bear Creek Ceremony Brandy made at the Bear Creek Vineyards, Lodi, sold after four and a half years in wood, is claimed by some to be the best of the California Brandies. Lejon Brandy made by Shewan-Jones and Korbel Brandy, both products of Lodi, are very good; and the Mattevista Brandy made by A. Mattei, Fresno, is another excellent Brandy. We make good Brandies in this country.

The label on a bottle, as mentioned earlier, is a wine's business card, and the buyer does well to give it serious attention. Added assistance in the matter of interpreting what one sees is given in *Guide to California Wines*[2] by John Melville, here quoted by Mr. Melville's generous permission: "The term 'produced and bottled' means that a minimum of 75 per cent of the wine has been produced, that is, fermented into wine, by the grower whose name appears on the label. 'Made and bottled' means that at least 10 per cent of the wine has actually been produced and that the balance has received some cellar treatment by the grower on the label, although it may not necessarily have been produced in his winery. . . . The term 'bottled' on the label means that the wine has merely been purchased and bottled."

[2] New York: Doubleday & Company; 1955.

In the early period of research, when the effect of environment on production first came to be understood, the staff at Davis divided the grape-growing districts of California into definite regions. The regional plan is climatic, Region I including the coolest portions of the state, and Region V the hottest. This plan, with its divisions into localities and its recommendations of the grape varieties best suited to each, is a most satisfactory pilot through the wine country. It must quickly be added that the structure only is of university inspiration. The comments on the wineries in each region and on the wines they make are taken from my notes. The wineries of California are legion, but it must be true that the main of their production is liked and consumed at home because it has a very sparse representation outside the state. The list of wineries, therefore, appearing in their regional positions, is limited to the extremely small number whose names are familiar to wine-buyers in the national market.

A familiarity with the grape varieties each plants is essential for effective use of the plan:

RED: The two greatest are PINOT NOIR and CABERNET SAUVIGNON, already mentioned. Lesser reds are GAMAY from Burgundy; PETITE SIRAH, from the Rhône Valley; BARBERA, REFOSCO, NEBBIOLO, GRIGNOLINO, CARIGNANE, and CHARBONO from Italy; and ZINFANDEL from an unknown source. Italian-type wine, made by and for the large Italian population in California and elsewhere, has almost a life of its own. Made pretty much in the homeland pattern, the wines are typically characteristic of their kind: rugged, friendly, and forthright.

WHITE: The greatest are the WHITE RIESLING, often called JOHANNISBERG RIESLING, responsible for the best of Germany; CHARDONNAY, frequently listed as PINOT CHARDONNAY, and PINOT BLANC, producers of the great white wines of Burgundy and Chablis; and SEMILLON and SAUVIGNON BLANC, found in the Sauternes, Barsacs, and Graves of Bordeaux. Also producing sound wines are SYLVANER, TRAMINER, and CHASSELAS, all of which carry into American wines the characteristics ascribed to them in the chapter dealing with Alsatian wines; FOLLE BLANCHE, the grape of the Cognac district in France, which has had a moderate success when grown in certain sections of California; CHENIN BLANC, which makes the delightful wines of the Loire Valley in France; GRAY RIESLING, a subordinate member of the White Riesling family; and MUSCAT, which makes the sweet dessert wines.

REGION I

GRAPES RECOMMENDED: Pinot noir and Cabernet Sauvignon, also Gamay in the reds; White Riesling, Chardonnay, and Sauvignon blanc in the whites. *The vineyards in this and in Region II should produce the best in dry table wines.*

Vineyards

Valliant, Hollister, San Benito County, is one of California's oldest wineries, now owned and operated by the Hiram Walker interests. Valliant lists Riesling and Johannisberg Riesling, Sauterne, Chablis, and a *rosé;* also Port, Sherry, and sweet and dry Vermouth. Special attention is paid to the Riesling varieties and to the making of Vermouth, which is quite good.

Martin Ray, Saratoga, Santa Clara County, has never fitted into any category in the wine-making business. It is surprising to find him even sharing a region with anyone else. He is a perfectionist. Early in his career he filled his cellars with the finest wines Europe could send him, and set his sights to the heights they had achieved, breeding his wines accordingly. He still drinks the great Europeans in comparison with his own, sometimes now with the satisfaction of looking down from his height to theirs. The vineyards are planted to three grapes: Pinot noir, Chardonnay, and Cabernet Sauvignon, and the wines they make are in a class alone, superior wines one hundred per cent varietal. They are always vintage wines, made only in the years when they pass his rigid standards, and they are expensive. They include two Champagnes, one a pale pink; varietal wines carrying the names of the grapes which make them; and the Pinot Noir Rosé mentioned above. Expansion is in the air in this region. Sparked by Martin Ray, the result of his long fight for quality standards and control for California wines, is a new project coming into reality near by—Mt. Eden Vineyards. Ownership of the undertaking rests in a group of enthusiastic admirers of good wine, who have pledged themselves to the production of wines of highest excellence.

Paul Masson Vineyards, Saratoga, makes a long list of wines, including a dozen of the table variety, and a *rosé;* Champagnes Brut, Extra Dry, and two pinks; and Port, Sherry, Vermouth, and Muscatel. The wines I have tasted are average for California, mainly blends, which statement quite possibly does not do justice to their plantings of noble vines. The Champagne Brut is listed among the best of this variety made in the state.

F. Korbel & Brothers, Guerneville, in the Russian River country, produces sparkling wines only, its Champagnes well known over a number of years. The firm passed out of family hands in 1954, but the former policy of wine-making has been continued. The Champagnes are bottle-fermented, and the best of them are Korbel Brut, a very dry wine, and Korbel Sec, somewhat more sweet. A Korbel Rouge and a pink Champagne are made also.

REGION II

GRAPES RECOMMENDED: Cabernet Sauvignon, and for standard wines, Petite Sirah and Refosco in the reds; and in the whites, Pinot blanc, White (Johannisberg) Riesling, and Sauvignon blanc; and for the making of standard wines, Semillon, Sylvaner, and Folle Blanche.

Vineyards

Inglenook and Beaulieu in Rutherford, Napa County, are next-door neighbors in the beautiful Napa Valley, and there is an air of spaciousness and ease about them, deriving from tradition and continuity of effort. As it happens, the only American wines of considerable age I have tasted in many years came from these two vineyards. One was a white wine from Beaulieu which would have held its own in comparison with a Montrachet, and the other, a California Sauterne from Inglenook, was a delightful wine, with qualities inherent in the original. Once again, promise of a quality we too seldom find.

Both vineyards grow the white varieties listed; each adds Chardonnay and Traminer; in the reds Pinot noir and Gamay; and various other grapes used primarily for blending purposes. Inglenook's Charbono and Gamay I've always liked; the Cabernet Sauvignon is a good wine, and the Napa Valley Pinot Noir is one of the better of its type. From this vineyard come a Pinot Chardonnay which is well spoken of, and a Semillon that has no complexity but is very agreeable. It's like a pretty, pale-blonde woman looking cool in a white frock, refreshing and undemanding.

There is a definite distinction at Beaulieu between the signature and the type wines. Beaumont, a vintage wine made of the Pinot noir, although not rated tops among its kind, steps into quite a different class from Beaulieu's B V Burgundy; the same is true of its Georges de Latour Private Reserve, a vintage Cabernet Sauvignon, and the varietal of the same name; and of Chateau Beaulieu versus Dry and Sweet Sauternes. The exception may be Beauclair, a vintage Riesling, which seems to me not quite to live up to the reputation given it, while B V Napa Valley Riesling is an unassuming wine but consistently pleasing. By people who appreciate this type of wine, Beaulieu's Beaurosé is given high marks, compared favorably with *rosé* wines wherever made. Both vineyards make what Californians call dessert wines and every other wine region in the world calls fortified wines—that is, Ports and Sherries.

Beringer Brothers and Louis M. Martini, St. Helena, Napa County, are both family concerns. Beringer is being run by the second and third generations, and the second generation of the Martini family is now a member of that firm. Beringer wines are blends in the main, their character, by design, set to a reliable standard, and the firm is best known for its white wines: Chablis, Moselle, Rhine, and Sauterne. It also makes two Bordeaux-type wines, one Burgundy, sparkling and dessert wines.

As recorded in an earlier edition of this book, Mr. Martini embarked some years ago on an ambitious planting program, some of the vineyards pushing into hilly country, which places the Martini family in a comfortable, or uncomfortable, position astraddle Regions I and II. The Louis Martini Mountain wines were born of this enterprise, and those I have tasted seem well worth the trouble. The Johannisberg Riesling and the Folle Blanche are pleasant wines, the Pinot Noir was judged the best in its group, and the Cabernet Sauvignon, light in body for this type of wine, was nevertheless given a good mark. A tasting of the last two explains why the name Martini is linked with red wines in the popular and popular-priced market, as the name Wente is with white. The firm makes a good Zinfandel, that brusque wine; several white wines, including a pleasant dry White Pinot; and a Chianti from a blend of its own. The Pale Dry Sherry has had favorable mention.

Almadén at Los Gatos in the Santa Clara Valley is operated by a company with which Mr. Frank Schoonmaker is associated. The firm has extensive plantings, constantly being increased, the grapes including Pinot noir, Traminer, and Chardonnay in addition to the area suggestions.

While the wines I have tasted were about average for California, two must be excepted: Almadén Grenache Rosé made from a Rhône grape of that name, and the Almadén Brut Champagne. Mountain Red and Mountain White seem to have little besides attractive labels to recommend them. Almadén is now making Sherry by the *flor* method and has introduced the Solera system. The best of the series so far produced is Almadén's California Solera Golden.

There is also at Los Gatos the Novitiate of Los Gatos. The winery works principally for the church, but a small number of table wines—among them Cabernet Sauvignon, Burgundy, sweet and dry Sauterne, Pinot Blanc, Chablis, a *rosé*—and Port, Sherry, and a Black Muscat can be found on the market. The novitiate has a fair amount of quality grapes in its vineyards, but my impression is that most of its wines are blends. The Black Muscat is an unusual wine, and I had noted the Burgundy as a commendable effort to reproduce this wine.

Charles Krug Winery, St. Helena, is another old property. Charles Krug, who died in 1894, made his wines there for almost half a century, and the Mondavi family—Cesare and his sons—is now carrying on. Of its wines, which include a White Pinot, Dry Semillon, Gray Riesling, Traminer, and Gamay, the Traminer has a special standing, adding to its agreeable qualities a delicate bouquet. The two lesser blends, Burgundy and Claret, are not recommended. The quality signature of this house is *Charles Krug*.

The Christian Brothers, Napa, is another of the Catholic brotherhoods busy at the ancient trade of wine-making. The wines, both red and white, are chiefly blends, the Cabernet Sauvignon the best of the group. The brothers also make a number of Sherries.

GRAPES RECOMMENDED: Barbera, Carignane, and Refosco in the reds, and Semillon and Sauvignon blanc in the whites.

Vineyards

Cresta Blanca, Wente Brothers, and Concannon, all of Livermore. All three firms make Sauternes principally, having large plantings of the essential grapes.

A famous old name in the industry, Cresta Blanca is now the property of Schenley Industries. Before Prohibition put a stop to such pleasures, the fine white wines made by Cresta Blanca were in almost all cellars worthy the boast. Since that time the wine has not regained its old reputation, but the Cresta Blanca company has continued to produce the pale or golden wines of the Sauternes type, reaching for quality. Added now are Semillon, dry and sweet, and a group of red wines of which the Cabernet seems the best. Cresta Blanca also markets Champagnes, and a number of Sherries which are among the best made in the state. These include Cresta Blanca Dry Watch, California Palomino, and Triple California Cream.

Wente Brothers, a big producer of white wines, has a considerable acreage of both Semillon and Sauvignon blanc, and some of its best wines are made of these two grapes. Wine-making at this vineyard is a careful and serious business, the search for quality constant. Chateau Wente is the best of the Sauternes made here; the Sweet Semillon is a light-colored flowery little wine, uncomplex, but direct, clean, and good. The last Dry Semillon tasted was sharp and bitter, surely not typical of this wine. The Gray Riesling and Pinot Chardonnay, both vintage wines, are mentioned favorably, and others to look for include a vintage Sauvignon Blanc and Pinot Blanc. The best wines made by the Wente Brothers are the varietals which carry a special label, as, for example, Wente Brothers Livermore Pinot Chardonnay. The blended wines are sold under the Valle de Oro label and are not recommended.

Concannon Vineyard, owned by Joseph Concannon, the son of the founder, with the third generation coming up, was a firm built primarily to supply wine to the Catholic Church, which it still does. However, it thrives commercially as well. The best of the wines, it seems to me, is Sauvignon Blanc, with the Chateau Concannon and Dry Semillon following closely. Concannon makes also Sherry and Port, but none has reached these shores for tasting.

NEW YORK

The Eastern section of the United States produces wines quite unlike those found anywhere else on the globe. While California has taken pride in wines made from its *vinifera* plantings, the Eastern Seaboard, because of difficult climatic conditions and destructive pests, has had to rely upon hybrids of native grapes whose *vinifera* characteristics were arrived at by deliberate crossings between the European species and the native varieties, or transmitted to the wild stock during the long period when the settlers' attempts to persuade the finer species to accept soil and climate ended invariably in failure. Latterly, newer varieties of Franco-American hybrids have been added to the plantings of the native hybrid group; and more recently still one of the great wineries began experimenting with plantings of *vinifera* grafted onto well-tested native roots. Their success is noteworthy, to say the least of it.

It has come to be accepted that our long indifference to wine was encouraged by the period, two hundred or more years, when no wine was made in the Eastern states because the vines brought from Europe succumbed too quickly to inaugurate an industry and the wild varieties had little appeal for the winemaker. The earliest serious attempt to make wines of native grapes came just before 1800, when a grape called the Cape, believed to be of South African origin, thrived and was planted extensively in Kentucky and later in Ohio. The Cape was at least part native, and when its identity was established it provided the first hope that drinkable wines could be made from the despised wild vines that were everywhere, growing along with the brambles. The Catawba soon followed the Cape, and when the first Nicholas Longworth, whose hobby was the wine business, used it as the basis for his vast plantings in

Ohio, thereby making it famous, the Eastern wine industry was on its way.

The Finger Lakes region of New York State seems especially designed for the growing of wine grapes. Not only are soil conditions suited to the vine, but the vineyards lying on the gentle east and west slopes above the lakes are exposed to the full sun, and protected by the waters from disaster by frost in late spring and early autumn. Here are four great wineries, giants all, which have been making wines for several generations.

Champagne was the first wine of consequence made in this area, and all of the wineries are large producers of Champagne. Their cellars, which hold bottles counted in the millions, resting quietly while the wine ages, are at once very like and totally unlike the famous caves of France. Whereas the French are truly caves, vaulted and dim, crossed by dark figures moving in semi-obscurity, the American cellars are of concrete and steel, clean and well-lighted, the busy workers protected by long white coats. At this point, however, contrast ends and similarity carries on. The stacks of bottles, many deep, rise to familiar heights, the years demanded for the making of this wine, accepted from the French, are not skimped, and production methods, in essence, are the same.

Machinery has eliminated many of the hand operations which one may still watch in wine-cellars in Europe, but machinery cannot and does not replace the skills of the vineyard specialists who graft and prepare cuttings for future plantings, who separate, plant, and prune, and in other ways stand as sentinel throughout the life of the vine. For in this business the grape is king and queen and the whole of the royal court.

All of the wine-growers spoke with a certain weariness of the tag "foxy" which is most prominently identified with the Concord grape. It may almost be said that the highest hurdle they have had to clear is that same grape. A prolific growth, it has found its way everywhere, into jellies, jams, and pop; and the smallest hint of kinship has sometimes caused a wine to be dismissed with "Oh—grape juice!" The effort to control this family flavor, aggressive and a bit startling to palates accustomed to the bland European sorts, is responsible for the unrelenting search for new grape varieties, and for the experiments with milder and less distinctive wines in blends. Progress has been slow, but it has been punctuated by small sensations which have brought satisfaction in all quarters, and with it new appreciation of the wines, and a wider acceptance.

Quick and generous credit is given to Mr. Philip M. Wagner of the Boordy Vineyards, Riderwood, Maryland, for the great part he has played in advancing the cause of good wine in this area. Skilled winemakers, Mr. and Mrs. Wagner also run their own experiment station. There the first of the French hybrids, the famous Seibels and certain of the Bacos, were tested, and cuttings were made available to the growers of the Finger Lakes vineyards for experimental additions to the native hybrids. There are now extensive plantings of these hybrids in the region, one firm including as much as seventy-five per cent in its blends.

For what they may be worth in the way of guidance for new friends of the wines of this region, the following opinions were jotted down after tasting a number from the native growths:

RED WINES: The best are made from NORTON'S SEEDLING, ISABELLA, CLINTON, and IVES. The Ives makes a dark heavy wine sometimes used in coloring the too pale blends. The only EUMELAN I tasted was a green wine and therefore gave little indication of its true worth. It had a queer double flavor, as if it planned to be sweet, then changed its mind.

WHITE WINES: DELAWARE, delicate, mentioned by the growers with special affection, makes a creditable wine somewhat resembling a Moselle in general quality, having a nice flavor and aromatic bouquet; CATAWBA, pale in color with a clean and rather flowery bouquet, clean in taste; ELVIRA, fair bouquet, very dry, sharp tangy taste and a slightly bitter aftertaste; NIAGARA, sweet and dry in nice balance, like the richer-type Alsatian wine; DIANA, a very dry clean wine on the astringent side, good with fish; IONA, another good one, nice bouquet, very dry, slightly hard finish which is characteristic of many Eastern wines; MOORE'S DIAMOND, primarily a table grape, the wine strong and a bit yeasty; VERGENNES, dry, uncomplex wine, with more of a grape-juice than a wine smell; DUTCHESS, clean and dry, a seven-year-old wine nicely smoothed out; MISSOURI RIESLING, no relation to the White or Johannisberg, so named because of a suggested resemblance, has some of the charm of a dry Alsatian, with a pleasant bouquet.

Certain of the grapes mentioned above appear in most of the Champagne blends, which are typically complicated and individual with each house. Delaware, Catawba, Elvira, Dutchess, and Isabella are said to be the best for this purpose. The Champagnes, including the pink and the red, miscalled Sparkling Burgundy, are, with the exception of some few California wines, the best of their kind made in this country. The sharpness of the native grape adds a nice tang to the low-acid and mild California wines that are used in most blends. Carbonated Champagnes and sacramental wines are also made, the labels plainly proclaiming their kind.

It is quite possible that good *rosé* wines are made in this region, but, as stated earlier in this book, I am not an admirer of this type of wine and any opinion expressed must therefore be suspect.

Vineyards

Widmer's Wine Cellars, Inc., is located in a valley at the southern end of Lake Canandaigua, at Naples, New York. The head of the firm is William Widmer, the son of the founder. Widmer's makes a large and varied group of wines, but is best known for varietals, named for the grapes which make them. In the New York State wineries the fifty-one per cent of a designated grape demanded by federal law is more than respected, and most of the varietal wines are unblended. Absolute assurance is given when a vintage date is attached, a guarantee that the wine is made from one variety grown in a single year.

Two of the most distinctive wines made by this firm are Riesling Auslese (made from selected clusters) and Riesling Spätlese (late-picked grapes). They are made from the Missouri Riesling, from grapes which are touched in the late autumn by the fungus called in the European wine areas the *noble mold*. Requiring, because of this happy accident, special treatment, they are made only in fortunate years and are always vintage wines. Pale in color, they are very dry, with a hint of fruit flavor quite new to the palate.

Note also Dutchess, a nice fish wine with an agreeable bouquet; the delicate Moselle-like Delaware; Niagara, a charmer, its dryness overlaid with a small sweetness; and Isabella, a dry wine, light red in color. These are joined by other varietals in several categories, appearing under their decorative names, many of them too dry for my taste; by European-type wines, not in a class with the varietals; by Champagne Brut and other sparkling and carbonated wines; and by sweet dessert wines, Vermouths, Ports, and Sherries. The last are aged by a unique method. In fifty-gallon white-oak barrels placed on the roof-tops in stacks four high, the wines weather for four years of heat, rain, frost, and snow, mellowing and developing the nutty flavor requisite in Sherry wine. The older aged wines are drawn off while the younger remain. The *Consumer Reports* for December 1959, in its classification of Sherries, listed Widmer's Special Selection New York Sherry among the top ten in the judging of Intermediate Sherries, the only one of the American varieties to be so honored in any of the listings.

Widmer's has developed a new type of *apéritif*, the paler called Lady Widmer Silver Cocktail and the richer Lady Widmer Golden Cocktail. Both are interesting departures in this classification, aromatic, lightly pungent, the Silver Lady seeming the better rounded of the two.

Great Western Producers, Inc., the former Pleasant Valley Wine Company of Hammondsport, New York, is the least impressive of the four great wineries from the point of view of dedication. The Champlin family, which founded the firm and maintained it for three generations, has terminated its interest, and the over-all impression now is one of big business. However, the firm takes pride in possessing U.S. Bonded Winery License No. 1, and equal pride in the Great Western Champagnes, which built the fame of this company. The best of these to my taste is Brut Special. Others are Special Reserve, less dry than the

first, and Extra Dry, which is the sweetest of the
three. The firm also makes Claret, Burgundy, and
Sauternes types, the last a blend containing part
Seibel 1000; also a *rosé*, Chablis, Rhine, and sweet
dessert wines; and Vermouth, Sherries, and Ports.
Great Western is celebrating a centennial anniver-
sary.

Gold Seal Vineyards, Inc.: At no great distance
from Hammondsport is the proud holder of U.S.
Bonded Winery License No. 2, formerly Urbana
Wine Company. The president of this firm is a wine-
wise Frenchman, Charles Fournier, who received his
training principally at Veuve Cliquot in France, and
whose signature Champagne, Charles Fournier Brut,
and the lively Fournier Nature, caused many of us to
sit up and straighten our hats. Both wines are dry,
distinctive, and good. Two additional wines developed under M. Fournier's personal direction are the
charming Delaware, dry-sweet in nice balance, and
Keuka Rosé, made from Franco-American hybrids.
Other wines made by this firm include several varietals; type wines: Burgundy, Claret, Sauternes, all of
them taking second place to the varietals; and Vermouth, Port, and Sherry. The latter are consistently
among the better made in this country.

Gold Seal is once again making wine from *vinifera*
cuttings grafted onto native roots. It is not the first
time this experiment has been tried. Indeed, its
history is so long and the failures so consistent and
painful that men came finally to say it couldn't be

done. The project is under the very personal direction of a German viticultural scientist, Dr. Konstantin Frank, who was associated for three years with the New York State Agricultural Experiment Station at Geneva. Dr. Frank has been with Gold Seal for enough years to make his grafts, raise his vines, and begin to make his wines. The plantings include Pinot noir, Cabernet Sauvignon, Chardonnay, Riesling, Traminer, Pinot blanc, and Pinot gris. Of the wines tasted, the Pinot Blanc and Pinot Gris, modest grapes seldom moving into the illustrious class, were entirely typical, engaging wines with charming bouquets. The Riesling and the Chardonnay were glorious, at once noble and soft. In a year or two we may expect to find examples of this collection on the market; and, one may add, praises be!

Taylor Wine Company, Hammondsport, perhaps the largest of this group, has suffered neither change of name nor change of personnel. It is run now by the third generation of the family, with the fourth coming up, and one feels its roots go deep and that there is little danger of dislodgment. Often spoken of as the most conservative among vintners, the Taylors have moved steadily forward in winery as well as in vineyard, being the largest planters of Franco-American hybrids. It is not generally realized that the effort to raise the quality of wine by bringing in new varieties or strengthening the old is carried on by individuals or in experiment stations throughout the wine world, but so it is; and some idea of the breadth of the activity of these people, called hybridizers for easy convenience, is given by the numbers attached to their plantings. One of the foremost, M. Seibel, was an individual, not an institution; yet the Taylors plant Seibel numbers 5279, 7053, 10,878 and 13,053; and white 5276 and 9110. In addition to contributing new dimension to the flavor of the wine, the hybrids have the advantage, for this area, of a partial immunity to plant diseases, and of being high in sugar with a medium to low acidity.

From its earliest days Taylor Wine has produced still wines, but latterly Champagne has become its heaviest seller. Its cellars are capable of holding three and a half million bottles. The Taylors make a Brut and a Dry Champagne, and a red Champagne which is bottle-fermented and has little in common with Sparkling Burgundy but the name. They are not so concerned with varietals, but make European-type wines, some of them blended with as much as seventy-five per cent of the Seibels; and they add Vermouth, Port, and Sherry, also a Seibel-blended *rosé*, said by lovers of *rosés* to be a delicate example of its type.

Several wine firms, well known over many years, have folded their tents. Paul Garrett and Company and its affiliate, Vineyardists, Inc., have moved theirs to Guasti, California, and acquired the Italian Vineyard Company founded by Secundo Guasti. The firm is now Garrett & Company. Still a family affair, run by the third generation, the company makes a number of kinds of wine, the best its Paul Garrett signature wines. The famed Virginia Dare is still made in the East.

H. T. Dewey and Sons of Egg Harbor, New Jersey, has closed shop, and the formerly well-known Champagne, Cook's Imperial Dry, is now made by Cresta Blanca Wine Company of California.

Of the Ohio wineries only one remains, the Meiers Wine Cellars of Cincinnati. The Boordy Vineyard operated by the Wagners is increasingly active, and a newcomer, High Tor Vineyards in Rockland County, New York, has gone into limited production. As regards these three, one hears of their wine and finds an occasional special mention of them, but coming up with actual bottles is disappointingly difficult.

The New York State Agricultural Experiment Station at Geneva remains a participant, vitally concerned with all the problems of vine-growing and wine-making. The station works closely with the wineries, each responding to whatever call or request the other makes. It is a nice kind of partnership.

One final note: considering the national picture, hasn't the cult for "dry" been exaggerated, becoming an obsession rather than a taste? And isn't the impossible being asked of our wine-makers?

In an effort to achieve a dry wine the result sometimes is more acid than dry—a superimposed acid one suspects, rather than a natural; and many times in this review, of wines made in the West as well as in the East, the thought has come that if a number of the wines had been allowed to retain some part of their natural sweetness, and with it a larger portion of the fruit flavor which is, or should be, responsible for the whole thing, the experience in many cases would have been less puckering and more pleasant.

CHAPTER NINE

THE PURCHASE, CARE, AND SERVING OF WINES

Go, you old fools, go learn how to drink.
He who knows how to drink is a wise man;
he who knows not how to drink knows nothing!

One last word: Never let a drunkard choose your wine.
You may be sure that he knows nothing about it. It is
only sober people who know how to drink.

—M. Constantin-Weyer
L'Ame du Vin

The first essential in the purchase of wines is a
reliable dealer. Having stated the principle, one must
add that the creature grows increasingly elusive.
Shops dispensing wines and liquors are numerous,
but investigation generally reveals them to be concerned chiefly with spirits, the stock of wine meager,
the information far from reliable. Search, then, for
a wine-shop, and insist on time for browsing and full
answers to questions.

A second essential is some familiarity with the
principal types of wine and the foods they best ac-

company. A third is acquaintance with the best years of each type, and the age at which each reaches peak. Unless you enjoy the harsh underdevelopment of young wines, take care that those you buy are properly aged, and if there be question, buy single bottles for taste-testing before investing in a case. And in the American market realize that the proudest and most dependable wines bear a special signature, and make choice from among them.

Do not feel that you must buy only expensive wines, but when you do buy them, see that they are vintage wines, marked with the vintage years. The year should appear on the label and be stamped upon the cork. Good bargains may often be found among the humbler wines if you choose wisely, and also among great wines of fair years. The non-vintage wines need careful selection but can be good. Vintage wines are as a rule more reliable.

It is pleasant to have fine wines for grand occasions, and it is very pleasant to have a reasonable variety of wines to choose from—not only one wine of each useful type, but several. A nice parallel could be made between the wines chosen for a cellar and the books selected for a library. A library worthy of the name should supply one with every sort of reading, suit all moods, provide books for relaxation and amusement, books of value and consequence, and also those for the passing hour, corresponding, in wine, to that interesting group which is served at eleven o'clock or at five. A wine-cellar, even a fairly small one, can be equally diverse. It is an entertaining idea to play with.

Never, if you can avoid it, buy a bottle of wine and carry it home for that night's dinner, particularly if it be a red wine. Wine suffers from being shaken up. Try to have a stock on hand, however small.

THE CELLAR

The first thing to decide in planning a wine-cellar is whether you want wines for keeping and aging or whether you expect to drink them up within a few months or a year. In other words, it is a matter of long- or short-term collecting.

The only proper wine-cellar for long-term collecting is underground, in a spot that is dark and dry, away from heating-plant and water-pipes and the vibration of motors or washing machines. Those who live in houses usually find it possible to wall off a corner of the cellar with hollow tile or other material that insulates against heat. The temperature most to be desired is about 55° Fahrenheit, winter and summer. It will naturally fluctuate, but the less it does so the longer your wine is likely to last. Extreme cold is as injurious to wine as extreme heat. If your cellar is too warm, your wine will mature more rapidly than it should, but even when cellar conditions are far from perfect, a good wine is likely to last for a considerable time.

For short-term collecting, a cool closet in your

house or apartment will do, and if no cool closet is available, it is better to store your wines with your dealer, removing them from time to time as needed, but allowing at least two weeks between the time you bring them home and the time you serve them.

The closet to be used for the storage of wine should be selected with care. The best location is in the center of the house or apartment where the temperature is the most even, and away from the elevator shaft or other sources of jarring motion. Tranquility is the thing above all others that wine enjoys. Wherever vibrations are likely to be felt, and this holds true for all types of storage, it is well to block the bottoms of your racks or shelves with small wooden strips.

In addition, the door of the closet should be kept closed. Since the temperature variation between a closed closet and the remainder of the house is considerable, a closed door is important for the protection of the wine.

It is possible to purchase racks ready-made, in sections, which are economical in space. Wooden shelves will do if they are strongly built, and shelves or racks should be attached securely to the wall. If you use shelves, movable bits of wood or cork will block the bottles against rolling. Another method is to nail to the edge of the shelf an upright piece that extends an inch and a half to two inches above the level of the shelf. Into this piece cut notches or grooves to receive the necks of the bottles.

If your cellar is large, you will want bins for the wines you store in quantity. These bins should show an opening about a foot square, and if the bottles are stacked upon each other, the lower row may be blocked with bits of wood or cork to avoid slipping and breakage.

Never let a bottle of still or sparkling wine stand upright. As soon as a wine is received, tilt the bottle cork-downwards, so that the wine is against the cork and no bubbles of air remain; then slowly lay it on its side with the center of the label up, and in such position that the cork is *entirely* wet on the inside all the time. With the exception of Vintage Port which must always lie on its side, the fortified wines can stand upright, although many informed wine-drinkers keep all wines lying on their side. There is no objection to storing wine in the original cases provided the cases lie flat. They should be opened on arrival to avoid disturbing the wine just at the time it is wanted.

The rule for storing wines in the cellar is as follows: Champagne and other white wines in the lowest bins or on the lowest shelves; red wines in the tier above; Ports, Sherries, and Madeiras higher still and standing upright or lying on the side, whichever is preferred. Brandies, whiskies, gins, and liqueurs at the top, upright.

A work-table, a corkscrew, and a decanting funnel are important items in the equipment of a proper cellar. The corkscrew should never be of bent wire.

It should be made of steel, should have a long shank and a wide bore, and should work on the leverage principle, so that corks may be drawn without a tussel that would disturb the wine. The decanting funnel is of glass and is so constructed as to direct the stream of wine against the inner wall of the decanter.

TEMPERATURE

The proper temperature of wine is a matter on which epicures disagree to some extent, but their disagreements are concerned with minor points. All agree that white wines should be chilled or iced and that red wines should be served at approximately the temperature of the room in which they are to be consumed. It is also generally agreed that Claret shows to advantage when it is a degree or two warmer than the dining-room, and that red Burgundy need not be so warm as Claret; but this is a mere shade of difference, hardly noticeable.

As to just how cold the various white wines should be, there is some contention. Champagne, it is agreed, should be thoroughly iced. And, in my opinion, the very sweet white wines, such as Château d'Yquem, Marcobrunner Trockenbeeren Auslese, or Tokay Aszu should be iced. Some people say the latter wines should only be well chilled, but the best-informed opinion, I think, is on the side of a moderate icing for these dessert wines. Rather poor white wines are improved by a thorough icing, extreme cold tending to conceal their faults. This applies to the ordinary ninth-rate Sauternes that certain head waiters, who know less than they ought to, recommend as an accompaniment to fish. It applies also to poor Chablis and poor Alsatian and Rhine wines. But a very fine dry white wine, a great Rüdesheimer, Steinberger, Montrachet, or Meursault, needs only to be well chilled to slightly below the proper cellar temperature of 55°. Too much icing impairs their flavor. If the bottle is put in the ice-box for an hour or so, it will be about right.

Sherry served before dinner as an appetizer might properly be chilled. While this practice is thought by some to be barbarous, it is recommended by the best Sherry authority I know.

"It would shock our grandfathers," he says, "but they lived in the period of semi-glacial mid-Victorian residences, whereas we live generally in too much heat. The Sherry decanter has stood probably in an overheated room and the wine is therefore likely to taste flat. By chilling it a trifle we freshen it, and bring it, really, to about the temperature of an old-time London dining-room."

Anjou and Touraine white wines should be drunk cold. Port and Madeira should be a few degrees cooler than the room, for freshness.

Good red wines taste better as you go on drinking them. White wines do not unless they started at the wrong temperature, as for instance, a Montrachet that has been too much iced.

SERVICE

Do not disturb wine more than necessary on its way from cellar to wineglass. This is particularly a rule to observe in handling red wines, which contain more sediment than white wines, and most of all it should be observed in handling very old wines. For fine red wines the change from the cool cellar temperature to that of the dining-room should be accomplished by moving the bottle to the dining-room a day ahead and letting it rest there, gradually acquiring the warmth of the room; and the bottle should be opened about two hours before dinner to give the wine a chance to "breathe." Ordinary red wines require less attention but should be brought to the dining-room early enough to permit them to reach room temperature.

The cradle. Lift a respected bottle of red wine carefully from the bin, and without turning or shaking it, place it in the basket or cradle from which it will later be served. The cradle may be of silver or of wicker. In it the bottle reposes on its side, the neck slightly uplifted.

Drawing the cork. When the cork is to be drawn, entirely remove the metal cap of the bottle, or the sealing-wax, and wipe the neck very clean. Hold the bottle very tightly with the left hand while opening it so that pressure of the corkscrew does not rotate the bottle, thereby disturbing the sediment. It is well also to place a napkin under the hand to avoid risk from broken glass. Particularly in opening Champagne heed this rule; also when drawing a tight cork with an old-fashioned corkscrew by main force.

If you do not use a cradle, slowly turn your bottle upright when you remove it from the bin. Thereafter keep it in that position, except when you gently tilt it to pour the wine.

When the cork is drawn, wipe the lip of the bottle with a clean napkin. If the cork is rotten and bits of it fall into the bottle, the wine should immediately be decanted and strained through fine cambric. The decanting funnel, mentioned in the discussion of wine-cellars, must be scrupulously clean, and so, of course, must the decanter.

The question whether to decant or not to decant is another famous controversial point. The British believe in decanting, and most gourmets of my acquaintance think they overdo it. There is a club in London where even Champagne is decanted. My own rule is never to decant unless it is absolutely necessary, and this, I find, is very seldom. From my point of view it is not only quite as satisfactory, but a little more pleasant, to serve wines from the bottles in which they have so long resided.

If for some reason you are obliged to decant, place a light behind the bottle-neck and pour steadily, but not too fast, avoiding any backwash in the bottle. At the first sign of sediment, stop pouring.

The host will be smart if he attends to the wine service himself and does not leave that function to a disinterested maid or butler. The wine should be served *before* the food it is designed to accompany or simultaneously with it. A wine delayed is as bad or worse than a sauce or gravy that comes when the dish is half eaten.

If red wine is spilled on a tablecloth or mat, immediately cover the spot with salt and rub gently. Later, stretch the cloth over a bowl and pour boiling water in a gentle stream through the stain.

GLASSES

No object, however beautiful in itself, is well designed unless it perfectly fulfills the purpose for which it was created. This is true of everything from a city to a hat. Invariably the best designs are those which are best reasoned, and this fact is nowhere better illustrated than in wineglasses.

Connoisseurs of wine in France and England have expressed their ideas on wineglasses in various books, and the uniformity of their opinions is striking. This is because they are reasoned opinions. All emphasize the fact that three of our senses are called into play in making the acquaintance of a worthy wine.

Sight. "The tasting of wine," writes Louis Forest, eminent Parisian gourmet, "begins, like love, with the eyes." We lift our wineglass and enjoy for a moment the rich hue of liquid gold or garnet, shot with reflected light. The color of the wine may best be seen through fair, transparent crystal, thin, untinted, and unornamented—for wine, in the belief of a wine-lover, is "its own best ornament." Colored wineglasses, it is said, were contrived long ago to conceal the cloudiness of poor wines. They are not in good taste. Lead-blown crystal polishes better than ordinary glass.

Smell. We bring our glass to the level of the nose and savor the fragrance of the grape. For this purpose no skimpy little glass, but a large one, *half or less than half filled*, is best suited. The wine is gently rotated in the deep belly of the glass as it "breathes" and releases essences, volatile and fruity, which float in the air space above the surface of the wine, delighting the olfactory nerves.

Taste. With our lips we touch the glass, meeting the ultimate enjoyment that resides in a good wine.

Just as tea tastes best when drunk from a thin china cup, or an old-fashioned cocktail from an old-fashioned cocktail glass, wines taste best to a wine-lover when drunk from a certain sort of glass. In the New York of 1933 no proper wineglasses could be found. The things on the shelves were strange misshapen objects, colored for the most part, and either lavishly cut, or clumsy and covered with heavy wen-like decorations. The destruction that was Prohibition seemed to have made a clean sweep; not only had we torn the wine grapes out of the vineyards, but we had as well destroyed all simple clear glass and, apparently, their molds with them. After a considerable search I took to drawing-board and pencil to design my own.[1] Into the designs went everything I believed a good wineglass should be: crystal, spacious but light, with a slender cylindrical stem and a clean round base, wide enough to give a firm footing on the table and free from awkward angles and protuberances. The stem on a wineglass is important. The hand holding a stemless glass conceals the lovely color of the wine and tends to warm white wine, which should be cold.

The designs that follow illustrate two of the most useful of the glasses in the set. The first is the all-service tulip-shaped glass, made in four sizes for wine, the smallest holding three ounces, and the largest, nine and one half ounces. The bowl of the glass is deep, and it is drawn in slightly at the top to encase the precious bouquet and yet leave room for the enjoyment of both bouquet and taste. This type of glass is correct for the service of any wine, the eight-ounce, shown in the drawing, being the smallest size recommended for red wines. Burgundian wine-lovers generally prefer a larger glass, often serving their great red wines in immense balloon glasses, which permit the bouquet to swirl about beneath the nose, held in by a slightly contracted rim. These are much like the balloon glasses used for fine old Cognac,

[1] The manufacture of the Julian Street Glassware was stopped by the war, and, painful to relate, was never resumed. The company controlling the molds lacked sufficient pride in the line to continue its making. As a guide in the purchase of glass, note the eight-ounce example on page 228. Designs very like it do exist, and may be considered all-purpose, for the serving of almost any wine.

which gains in flavor and bouquet from being warmed by the cupped hands in which the glass is held.

The second design is of the Champagne flute. This glass is deceptive, being nothing like so large as it looks. It holds only eight ounces, but gives the appearance of the open generosity that should never be absent from the service of Champagne. The morning-glory type of glass—the small four-ounce size for Sherry, Madeira, and Port, and the larger for Champagne—is suitable only for wines of small bouquet or for those in which bouquet is of secondary importance.

Where several wines are served, the glasses are ranged to the right of one's place at table, with the water goblet on the left, the large glass for the principal wine coming next, and the other glasses following in a descending scale of size, with the smallest on the right. A handsome table, set with a fine array of sparkling glasses, is a pleasant thing to look upon, but the glasses are at once a promise and a warning. Drink sparingly of the first wines in order to enjoy the last.

THE ALL-SERVICE TULIP-SHAPED GLASS

THE CHAMPAGNE FLUTE

CHAPTER TEN

FOOD AND WINE

Oh, how blest for bounteous uses
Is the birth of pure vine-juices!
Safe's the table which produces
   Wine in goodly quality.

—JOHN ADDINGTON SYMONDS
*(Translation of Latin Song of Wandering
Students—twelfth century)*

It is rather extraordinary, if one compares them
all, how uniform have been the conclusions of ex-
perienced and conscientious people as to the harmony of certain bouquets and flavors in wine with
the taste and scents of certain foods. For wine is a
thing of flavor, a flavor as strikingly definite and
varied as any to be found in food, and it is only by
achieving harmony between them that one is able to
enjoy both to the fullest extent.

This simple rule does not find favor with the experts, as anyone knows who has followed the wine
and food publications in the last ten years or so. In
fact, the advice they give is exactly the reverse, in
effect: "Don't be bluffed, drink anything you like.
Follow your own taste." That this advice is bad many

an eager new wine-drinker must have learned to his sorrow when, stopping on his way home from the office, he bought a bottle of just any wine, shook it up well, and had it that night with his dinner.

We have long since accepted without fuss the necessity for care in combining food flavors. We don't put mint sauce on a broiled steak and we don't drink hot chocolate with fish. Arriving at happy alliances between wine and food is nothing like so complicated as hunting out and preparing the sauce best suited to whatever dish is under construction—no *more* complicated, surely, and much more diverting. It is a delight to work out pleasant combinations; and to stumble onto perfections in flavor can raise any meal to the memorable. Since there are so many hundreds of wines, the delight is endless, and the nice combinations one can get are almost equally endless.

If a wine is to be drunk by itself to quench thirst or with a chunk of bread or with bread and cheese, yes, drink just any wine, because almost any wine will do; but wine has another and more exalted place. It belongs to the dinner table, and if the diner hopes to enjoy his dinner, he will be wise if he gives the choice of his wine *at least the same degree of thought and attention he has given to his food.* Food is the tune, wine the accompaniment. Each must be right for the other.

To go back for a moment to taste, this absolute arbiter of selection. It is not a thing one can know in a moment. It requires many bottles—not, however, all at one sitting—and a conscious effort to remember the color, flavor, and bouquet of each wine tasted to reach a decision as to preference for any type. A good plan for a young person seeking to know his taste in wine is to lay down a cellar of a dozen bottles or so, selecting at the start of the experiment wines which harmonize with favorite foods. Buy single bottles only, let the wines rest and begin to experiment. Replace those used up, bottle by bottle, varying the choice, and allow the replacements to rest. Soak the labels off each empty bottle, paste them in a notebook and include an opinion of the wine. In a few months you will understand what taste in wine means, and you will have, in addition, a record of that taste as it changes. Because taste does change, and in the matter of the development of our taste in wine, most of us have followed pretty much the same pattern. We have begun by liking Sauternes; gradually Sauternes have come to seem a little cloying and we have branched out through the semisweet into the dry. Ultimately we have learned what others have learned and set down before us: That while taste varies, the variation is within the type and seldom outside it. None of us could be happy eating a steak over which mint sauce had been poured, and likewise, the only really perfect wine to serve with oysters is Chablis.

The list of tested kinships between wine and food which follows may be considered as combined with suggestions for a small cellar—as giving the novice a place to start. The problem of choice here is a fine one, based not only upon preference but as well upon the weight of one's pocketbook. One often hears it said, it seems with truth, that we cannot fully appreciate wine without knowing the great in each kind as well as the small. Great wines are costly and few of us can afford them in quantity, but it is always reassuring to have on hand a few single bottles of fine wine, cached away in the cool and the quiet, awaiting their share in one's big days.

Apéritif: When no cocktail is served, Madeira, Sherry, and Vermouth have come to be accepted; however, a light white wine is uniquely right at this point, and the choice is wide: Quincy, Muscadet, and Vouvray from the Loire; Traminer and Gewürztraminer, or if a drier wine is preferred, Riesling or Sylvaner, American or Alsatian; light Moselles; Niagara or Delaware; Fendant or Johannisberg from Switzerland; or a *rosé*, import or American. If the supper to follow is to be informal, plan the menu so that the glasses may be transferred to the table, and the wine continued. For festive occasions, especially if no other wine is to be served, Champagne lovers often elect to begin and continue with that wine. If you are of their number, consider an American —there are many good ones; or make choice from among the French companies listed in the Champagne chapter.

Soup: Wine and soup have little in common unless the soup be clear consommé. Serve then an Amontillado Sherry or Sercial Madeira. The soup may well be flavored with the wine.

Fish: Most of the wines in the *Apéritifs* listing combine pleasantly with fish. Add Chablis, provided an honest wine is procurable, Fournier Nature, the Dutchess and Riesling varietals of New York State; California White Pinot or Chardonnay; a dry Swiss wine; light Rhines, slightly on the rich side for the sweeter sorts of fish; and white Burgundies up to and perhaps including a Chevalier-Montrachet.

With Light Meats and Poultry: The list is almost as long as one can draw, beginning with Pouilly Fuissé, Beaujolais, and other South Burgundians; the stouter among the wines of the Loire; a not too important French Claret, Taylor's Claret, Cabernet Sauvignon, Pinot Noir, and Chardonnay from California; semi-dry Rhines, Spanish Rioja, a full-flavored Swiss or one of the *rosés.* Equally well with certain entrées go the great white Burgundies, Montrachet, Meursault, and Corton Charlemagne; or Châteauneuf-du-Pape, or the fine white Rhône wine, Hermitage; or Champagne. These rich white wines make a splendid accompaniment for sweetbreads and creamed lobster, and also guinea hen, quail, and even curried dishes if the curry be very light. With lamb try a Claret from the commune of

Saint Julien, one of the Léovilles, Gruaud-La-rose, Langoa-Barton or Beychevelle; or if a spicier variety appeals, choose a Burgundy from the Côte de Beaune, from Pommard or Volnay.

With Simple but Hearty Meat Dishes: District Médocs, Italian wines, including Grignolino and Charbono, California Zinfandel, Gamay, and the heavier Spanish wines.

With Red Meat and Game: At this point one goes all out, or as far in that direction as is possible. Médoc of a good year and *cru* or an authentic Cabernet Sauvignon is the lightest wine that harmonizes with red meat or rich game; better a great wine of the First *Cru,* or one of the Châteaux Ausone, Cheval Blanc or Pétrus; as well would be a rich red Rhône; and best of all a noble Côte d'Or Burgundy or Martin Ray's Pinot Noir, stepping up the wine as the occasion demands.

With Salad: No wine with salad if vinegar is used in the dressing. Lemon juice is a good substitute for vinegar. If salad is brought on as a separate course in a dinner party, continue the preceding red wine and if possible serve a mild cheese. Cheese is perhaps the most perfect of all foods with a red wine, but unless it is mild it over-whelms wine and can completely submerge exquisite old ones. *Fois gras* and the game patés follow cheese in preference.

With Dessert: This is the only place where the great

naturally sweet wines, the Sauternes, the Trockenbeeren Ausleses, and the Tokay Aszus, are at
home. All of them are costly. Substitution, understandably not in kind, may be made from
among the dessert wines of New York State and
California: the wine called Tokay, for example,
which has no association with the great Hungarian but crops up on both coasts; or the Black
Muscat made at the Novitiate of Los Gatos, or
one of the Muscatels of California. The dessert
should not be too sweet, allowing the wine to
mount above it. A nut soufflé flavored lightly
with the wine to be served is perfection. Try
also the richer fortified wines with fruit, nuts,
and raisins. Madeira is especially good when
served in this way; and there are the rich cream
Sherries.

Odd Hour or Occasion: For light summer lunches, a
choice from among the wines listed under *Apéritifs;* for picnics, a white wine which travels well,
to be cooled in a brook: a Pouilly Fuissé, or
again a choice from the *Apéritifs* suggestions;
with chicken sandwiches, a light Moselle, a Delaware or Niagara; with fondue any of the wines
of Switzerland; at five o'clock with thin cucum-
ber sandwiches, a sweetly scented wine of Germany or Alsace.

All of the wines listed above, their origin, type, and
position in the hierarchy, are described in the text of
the book.

If you are fortunate enough to have fine wines, you may find it advantageous to follow the practice of European gourmets and build your dinner around your wines, rather than ordering your wine to fit your meal. The thing to strive for in planning a dinner is an interesting combination of food flavors and wine flavors.

There are certain foods wine seems not to favor: hors d'oeuvres have a vinegar base and vinegar is the enemy of wine; also, wine may be drunk with an egg dish, but no wine is at its best with eggs. Jellies or sharp sauces will ruin the flavor of any wine. Some people recommend red wines with fish, but since every wine country in the world makes numbers of white wines which are natural complements to fish, it seems unnecessarily brash to risk even part of one's pleasure.

Weather is a factor in one's choice of wine, but instinct is a safe guide here. Certainly nothing is more unpleasant on a hot day than a glass of heavy wine. And the purists permit no smoking until after dinner, holding that it has a noxious effect on the palate.

Finally, wine brings a wholly new aspect to good living. The person who finds his highest pleasure in dining quietly and well in the company of a few congenial friends collects wines as he collects art objects, and not a little of his interest is due to the fact that, unlike his art objects, his wines don't "stay put." For wine is a living thing, subject to change, like a person, almost to moods. In an effort to cut it down to size, several writers have called wine a farm product. So it is, comparable in making to cheese in its intricate and various requirements. Ninety per cent of the wine made in the world is ordinary, drunk where it is grown. The treatment given the remaining ten per cent, beginning with the quality and care of the vines, is such as to place certain of the resulting wines in a class with the world's sublime creations. Dr. Maynard Amerine, writing in the Winter Number of the *Wine and Food Quarterly* for 1942, says of wine that it is nobler than any mere commodity that we buy or sell, which establishes its place in history and explains its permanence and stability.

Storage of Wine—Addendum: The shelves of the apartment wine-cellar should be built all the way across the closet and just high enough to slip in the bottles. In this way any bottle can be removed without disturbing the others.

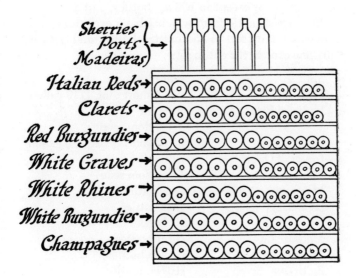

Sherries
Ports
Madeiras →

Italian Reds →
Clarets →
Red Burgundies →
White Graves →
White Rhines →
White Burgundies →
Champagnes →

THE SIZES OF WINE BOTTLES

The larger the bottle, the better the wine. Identical wine tastes better when drunk from a quart bottle than from a pint, or from a Jeroboam than from a quart. It used to be said by wine-lovers who frequented the Restaurant Voisin, in Paris, which had the best cellar of any restaurant in Europe, that no one had ever tasted Château d'Yquem until he had drunk it from a Magnum.

I have not seen an Imperial Pint or an Imperial Quart in many years, except in whisky bottles, and a Jeroboam is the largest bottle from which I have ever drunk wine. Collectors are fond of the outsize bottles and occasionally one can see the entire set:

Split	half pint
Pint	usual short pint, 1/10 gallon
Imperial Pint	full pint (seldom seen)
Quart	usual short quart, 1/5 gallon
Imperial Quart	full quart (seldom seen)
Magnum	two bottles
Jeroboam	four bottles
Rehoboam	six bottles
Methuselah	eight bottles
Salmanazar	twelve bottles
Balthazar	sixteen bottles
Nebuchadnezzar	twenty bottles

On this subject the Honorable Henry French Hollis of Paris once wrote: "Good vintage years are those which have rain enough to bring the grapes to full size, sun enough in August and September to develop sweetness and flavor, and atmospheric conditions, including dryness and temperature, suitable for proper fermentation of the juice."

No two vintage charts are identical. Made by people of sensitive palate, tasting and comparing many wines of all years, the difference between the various conclusions is understandable; also it is very slight—for example, one authority will consider the wines of a specific district and year to be very good while another will call the same wines great.

A thing to understand about the wines of each year is that their quality in all districts is fairly uniform. The peninsula of Europe is no great land mass, and while there can be sudden onslaughts of frost or hail, these calamities touch restricted areas only. When Europe has a rainy summer all of the wine-growing regions are affected. Thus we see that the years 1943, 1945, 1947, 1949, 1952, 1953, 1955, and 1959 produced very good or great wines in all districts, 1948 especially good Clarets and white Burgundies, 1950 fair to excellent wines in all but Champagne, and 1957 fair wines throughout, slightly above the average in Burgundy and in the German districts.

The small wines of most wine-growing countries, those of the Loire, the Beaujolais, and the lesser breeds both red and white wherever found, should be drunk young because they are bottled young. The great reds, and white wines of equal stature from Sauternes, Burgundy, and Germany, develop a longer time in cask before bottling and require additional age to reach perfection.

TABLE OF VINTAGE YEARS
SINCE 1943

	BORDEAUX RED (CLARET)	BORDEAUX WHITE	BURGUNDY RED	BURGUNDY WHITE	CÔTES DU RHÔNE	RHINE AND MOSELLE	CHAMPAGNE
1943	Good	Great	Good	Great	Great	Good	Good
1944	Fair	Fair	Poor	Poor	Fair minus	Fair minus	Fair minus
1945	Great	Very great	Very great	Great	Great	Great	Great
1946	Fair minus	Fair minus	Fair	Good	Fair	Fair	Fair minus
1947	Very great	Very great	Very great	Very great	Very great	Great	Very great
1948	Good	Fair	Good	Good	Fair	Good	Fair
1949	Great	Good	Very great	Great	Great	Very great	Great
1950	Very good	Fair	Fair	Great	Very good	Good	Fair minus
1951	Poor	Fair minus	Poor	Fair minus	Fair	Poor	Poor
1952	Great	Very good	Very great	Very great	Very great	Great	Very great
1953	Very great	Great	Great	Great	Great	Very great	Very great
1954	Fair	Poor	Fair	Fair	Good	Poor	Fair
1955	Great	Great	Great	Great	Very great	Good	Great
1956	Fair minus	Fair	Poor	Fair	Fair	Poor	Poor
1957	Good	Fair	Very good	Very good	Good	Very good	Fair
1958	Very good	Very good	Fair	Good	Very good	Good	Fair
1959	Very great	Very great	Very great	Great	Very good	Very great	Very great

ALCOHOLIC STRENGTH OF
WINES AND BRANDY

Champagne	12 to 13%
Red Bordeaux (Claret)	9 to 11%
White Bordeaux (Sauternes, Barsac, Graves, etc.)	9 to 12%
Burgundy (Côte d'Or)	12 to 14%
Burgundy (southern region)	11 to 14%
Rhône	12 to 14%
Rhine and Moselle	9 to 13%
Sherry and Madeira	18 to 22%
Port	18 to 23%
Tokay { Aszu	12 to 14%
{ Szamorodni	16 to 17%
Cognac[1]	30 to 72%

Fluctuation in the alcoholic strength of natural wines results from: (1) the nature of the soil itself, (2) the strength of the wine in any given vintage year, and (3) the age of the wine. A young natural wine is likely to be stronger in alcoholic content than a very old wine, but fine old wine tends to gain in delicacy of flavor and bouquet.

[1] Cognac Brandy when first distilled has an alcoholic strength of from 68 to 72%. By aging in the barrel for many years this alcoholic strength may gradually be reduced, but the usual practice is to reduce by blending the high-proof Cognac with a Cognac of lower proof, the latter having been "broken down," as the process is called, in part by age and in part by the introduction of water, slowly, in small quantities over a period of time. It does not do to add water brutally or to mix it direct with the very strong young Brandy. It must be introduced only in the form of a blend composed chiefly of Brandy. By this process Brandy may be made smooth much earlier than by the process of aging in the barrel. The latter, however, is the better process.

INDEX

aboccato, defined, 149
Ackerman, 103
Ackerman-Laurance, Loire, 39
Adams, John, 156
adulterants, test for, 112
Aeschylus, 181
Africa, 25
age in wine, 30-1, 39-40, 55-6, 76, 86, 88, 90, 101, 103, 105-6, 125, 129, 131-2, 145, 164-5, 169, 175, 241-2
Albana, Italian, 150
alcohol in wine, 26, 30; table of alcoholic strengths, 243
Aleatico, Italian, 151
Algerian wine, 93
Allen, H. Warner, 5
Almadén Vineyards, and wines, 199-200
Aloxe-Corton, comm., of Burgundy, 75-6, 94-5; wines: Les Vercots, 76; *Supr., First Grths.*, Corton, Corton Clos du Roi, 80; *First Grths.*, En Charlemagne, La Vigne au Saint, Les Bressandes, Les Grèves, Les Perrières, Les Pougets, 81
Alsace, wines of, 106-8, 194; age for drinking, 106; grapes and types of wine from, 107; vintage years, 108; temp., for drinking, 221; with food, 107, 233, 236; districts of: Ammerschwihr, Barr, Colmar, Eguisheim, Epfig, Gertwiller, Guebwiller, Kayserberg, Mittlewihr, Molsheim, Obernai, Ribeauvillé, Riquewihr, Thann, Turckheim, Wintzen-

Alsace (*continued*)
heim, Wolxheim, Zellenberg, 107-8; Riquewihr-Riesling, 108; American, 194, 206-7
Alsace-Lorraine, 26, 106, 206-7
Amalgaire, Duc d', 9
America: drinking habits in, 17-22; Madeira, 18; early vine growing, 18-20; phylloxera, 30; *see also* "The Wines of the US"
America, North and South, wines of, 25
Amerine, Maynard, 191, 238
Amontillado Sherry, 155
Amoroso Sherry, 156
Anacreon, 4
Anjou, div., of Loire Valley, wines of, 29-30, 102-4, 145; best-known growths, 103-5; temp. for drinking, 221; with food, 233-4, 236
Anne, Queen of England, 16
apéritifs recommended, 144, 155, 159, 166, 191, 209, 233-4, 236
Appellation Contrôlée, discussion of, 93-7
Apple-Brandy, 114
Arbois, Jura wine, 101, 109
Armagnac, *see* Brandy, 114
Arsac, comm., of Bordeaux, 60
Artisans, cru de, 48
Assmannshäuser, Rheingau red, 127
Asti Spumante, Italian, 146, 151
Auslese, 70; also *Feine Auslese, Hochfeine, Feinste Auslese*, defined, 120
Ausonius, 7

INDEX

INDEX

INDEX

INDEX

INDEX

INDEX

INDEX

INDEX

INDEX

INDEX

INDEX

INDEX

INDEX

JULIAN STREET was born in Chicago on April 12, 1879. He attended the Chicago public schools and a preparatory school in Canada. He became a newspaper reporter at nineteen, and at twenty-one was married and in charge of the dramatic department of a New York evening paper. He reviewed the first American performance of *Floradora*, for which he prophesied failure. After a brief fling at advertising, he went to Europe with Booth Tarkington and Harry Leon Wilson to try his luck at articles and fiction for American magazines.

From 1906 on, Street wrote voluminously for magazines and published novels, collections of short stories, and travel books. He collaborated with Tarkington on *The Country Cousin*, the play that provided Alfred Lunt with his first Broadway vehicle.

Street was long interested in the twin arts of wining and dining. He once said of the present book that it was "designed to give all necessary information about wines that can be obtained without a corkscrew."

Julian Street died on February 19, 1947.

A. I. M. S. (MRS. JULIAN) STREET was born January 1, 1899, in Tacoma, Washington, and educated there, completing her studies at the University of Mexico and the American Academy of Dramatic Arts in New York.

Mrs. Street came of drinking age simultaneously with Prohibition, but soon after her marriage to Julian Street in 1930 her knowledge of wines grew rapidly as she worked as his editorial and research assistant on the writing of *Wines* and as merchants from all over the world brought samples to their home. Mr. Street had high regard for his wife's knowledge and it was his confidence that encouraged her to undertake the first revision of *Wines* after his death. She has continued his work with the publication in 1959 of *Table Topics*, a compilation of wine and food pieces left by Mr. Street, and with the present up-to-date edition of *Wines*.

A NOTE ON THE TYPE

THE TEXT of this book is set in *Caledonia,* a Linotype face that belongs to the family of printing types called "modern face" by printers—a term used to mark the change in style of type-letters that occurred about 1800. Caledonia borders on the general design of Scotch Modern, but is more freely drawn than that letter.

Composed by Publishers' Composition Service, Inc., Brattleboro, Vermont. Printed and bound by H. Wolff, New York. Paper manufactured by S. D. Warren, Company, Boston.